Accelerated Reader
Level 4.8

I'll Ask You Three Times, Are You OK?
By Naomi Shihab Nye
The author is a poet and visiting teacher. Each chapter
is a recollection of experiences she had while riding
with someone in her world travels or driving herself.
I thought someone's experiences as a traveler would
be interesting but they were not. Although there were
several stories that were ok, most were not. In fact, the
best one was the last chapter and by then it was too
late. I would not recommend this book but if someone
were to purchase it, it's more appropriate for upper
middle school.
-Deb Daehnke, WSC

I'll ask you three times,

are you
OK?

Everything feels tinged with the sting
and prickle of loving.
—Noël Hanlon

NAOMI SHIHAB NYE

I'll ask you three times,

are you

OK?

Tales of driving and being driven

GREENWILLOW BOOKS
An Imprint of HarperCollinsPublishers

The text type is 12-point Grajon.

Page 242 constitutes an extension of this copyright page.

Library of Congress Cataloging-in-Publication Data
Nye, Naomi Shihab.
I'll Ask You Three Times, Are You OK? Tales of Driving and Being Driven
/ Naomi Shihab Nye.
    p. cm.
"Greenwillow Books."
ISBN: 978-0-06-085392-1 (trade bdg.) ISBN: 978-0-06-085393-8 (lib. bdg.)
1. Nye, Naomi Shihab—Travel. 2. Voyages and travels—Juvenile literature.
I. Title.
PS3564.Y44I45 2007 811'.54—dc22 2006036548

First Edition 10 9 8 7 6 5 4 3 2 1

 Greenwillow Books

In memory of Trinidad Sanchez, Jr.

Contents

In Eldorado, Texas, the lovely western ranch town unexpectedly popular with polygamists, I saw a hand-lettered sign in a triangular park that read, "A HAPPY PERSON IS ONE WHO ENJOYS THE SCENERY ON A DETOUR."

Introduction

IN SYRACUSE, NEW YORK, A LIGHT MIST IS hovering at 5:15 A.M. I like it here. Nice friendly people and lots of old buildings. Just my style. I wish I were staying longer. A taxi driver has loaded another person's luggage into the trunk, thinking he's the one who called for a ride, not me. I stand with my red suitcase staring at his car. The driver says, "Are you room three-sixteen? Oh, I thought he was." He hoists the man's luggage back out of the trunk and loads mine instead. The other passenger sniffs, "I am waiting for a *limousine,* not a taxi."

This gives the taxi driver a big laugh as we pull out of the lot. "He'll pay a *dear buck* for a limousine! Ha-ha! And it's not a long trip to the airport! What a waste of money!"

I'm remembering a time the driver of a shared taxi in Palestine gave my father's luggage to another passenger when the older man disembarked first. My dad, sitting up front, didn't notice his own bag had left the car. Upon arrival at his destination, he was stuck with the elder's suitcase filled with white pilgrimage-to-Mecca clothes—not exactly my dad's daily wardrobe. He spent *days* looking for that old man so they could exchange suitcases again. He had all kinds of adventures along the way.

Now I ask my early driver, "Are you from Syracuse?"

He says, "Proud to say, I lived here all my days—sixty-three years!"

Then he says firmly, in the serious, rehearsed tone of a person giving a speech, "I'll answer any Syracuse questions you have, but before that I need to tell you something important. Since you're a lady and we're alone, and it's dark, I'll ask you three times on the way to the airport: Are you okay? Just to make sure you feel safe and secure. We're living in strange times, and I want you to feel very comfortable. Okay?"

"Okay. Very nice of you."

We're passing dark factories. Some look abandoned. One shadowy building has a repainted Uneeda Biscuit 5 cents sign on its side. Yesterday I ate lunch at the Lucky Moon and Stars Café. Their specialty soup was called Greens & Beans. It is really hard to be lonely very long in a world of words. Even if you don't have friends somewhere, you still have language, and it will find you and wrap its little syllables around you and suddenly there will be a story to live in.

He says, "Are you okay?"

"I'm just great. A little early for bopping around, but I'm fine."

"Excellent. What else do you want to know about Syracuse?"

"How has it changed in your lifetime?"

"See this highway we're on? It cut my city right in half. That's a hard thing."

"I'll bet it took a lot of good buildings away."

"Sure did. When I was little we did all our shopping downtown. We had five theaters downtown. Now we have one. The people made a decision to shop at the malls in the suburbs instead of downtown, and more and more malls grew up. It's a decision, you know. A decision people make."

"I hate it. I prefer to shop downtown. We live downtown in my city."

"Where's that?"

"San Antonio."

"How many people?"

"More than a million."

"We're 141,000."

"Wow, Syracuse feels much bigger."

"I know—it's spread out." We stare off to both sides at all the twinkling lights. Then he says, "Are you okay?"

"I am just fine, thanks!" I continue, "Well, one nice thing is when empty buildings turn into something again—that reuse factor. A lot of old buildings where we live are turning into loft apartments right now and young people are moving into them. That's a good thing. It helps downtown stay alive."

"Sure it does. Good trend. It's happening here, too. Very hopeful. Like an injection."

This makes me laugh. I like the image of giving a city an injection. I think most cities need a whole cycle of injections by now. I'm starting to wish the airport were in Albany, hours away. He keeps both hands on the wheel. I would bet money he *never* exceeds the speed limit.

I say, "I like Syracuse a lot. It felt interesting here. I walked around."

"I'm glad you like my city. What's your airline again?"

"Delta."

"Excellent. We're already there. See how fast it was? Not too much traffic this time of day. Are you still okay? Were you okay the whole time?"

He's jumping out to unload my luggage. He's wearing a fresh white shirt and dark pants and a little brimmed cap like Greek fishermen wear. I could almost hug him.

But I stuff a tip into his hand and say, "I was very okay."

I don't know when it hit me that what happened in the margins, on the way to the destinations of any day, might be as intriguing as what happened when you got there. I used to think a lot about what happened on the way to school even while I was at school. It distracted me, but I was grateful for it. I would close my eyes and picture walking up the hill between the spooky trees, around the bends of streets, staring at houses in varying states of chaos, disrepair, or care, wondering hard about the few neat people, talking to squirrels, birds, dogs, and cats, trying to revive or rescue hurt animals, picking up lost buttons and papers and lovely leaves, harboring questions about mysterious families who never came out of their houses, inventing scenarios—all this fascinated me much more than economic facts about faraway France, or abstract equations.

Walking in the hall at school, on the way to recess or lunch or the library, one also learned crucial necessities—who liked whom, who had broken a leg, who had broken up, who was suddenly wearing sackcloth, etc.

Riding around neighborhoods in the evenings, in the backseat of anyone's car, before shades were dropped or curtains closed, one might spy on other families through their lit windows—seeing a piano, a painting, a table set for dinner—my overactive nostalgia-tinged brain wanted to meet them. Weirdly, I missed them even before I met them.

My mother used to tell me when I went somewhere, "Please leave your foolishness at home." But how could I do that? It was stuck to me. Sort of like the faded NO HOPE GOAT RANCH sign tacked to a fence we passed one time in southern Colorado.

To this day, riding in taxis between places often seems as memorable as the places on either end. I suffer the delusion that I too am a taxi driver. My passengers are groceries, books, friends. I do not want to go home yet.

The writers who meant the most to me in high school and college had wildly variant opinions about traveling. Henry David Thoreau thought we didn't need to leave our own backyards or nearby woods. Jack Kerouac roared back and forth across the country in his friend's old car. His most famous book was *On the Road*. I loved them both. Most teenagers I know have a mixture of desires—to go, go, go, but also to stay cozily contained, wherever one is comfortable. Many haven't found that place yet and keep looking for it. Driving up new roads, peering out the windows . . .

For every little tale in this book, there are hundreds of others untold. I did not tell about the taxi driver in Guatemala who roared like a race car driver up and around the mountain roads at midnight (he did not seem intoxicated, however), slowing down only slightly when we begged him to, who confirmed that the woman we saw outside our taxi, rising up in a flowing see-through chiffon gown, like a yellowed glowing curtain, was indeed the ghost of a mother whose children had perished off that cliff years before. I can't remember now if she had pushed them, or if they were doomed passengers of another wild auto ride, but I saw her myself with wide-awake eyes and so I will always believe. *A ghost.* Rising out of the dark. The taxi driver said she was a famous ghost and everyone had seen her. My mother saw her, too.

I did not tell here about the taxi in Nepal that also terrified us, on which I made a pledge to stay on flat land for the rest of my days, or the taxi drive in Egypt that ended up with us in a stone house by the pyramids, delivering a wristwatch to a family we didn't know, from someone we had met on a plane, eating the largest meal of our lives when we weren't even hungry, and then our little son deciding to clean the kitchen floor with a broom and a mop— while I stared out the window, thinking, "There is no end to the possibilities on this planet." I didn't tell about Carefree Highway in Phoenix or the faded HOLINESS IS BEAUTIFUL sign hand-lettered in blue on an old building in Memphis. I did not tell about driving cross-country with a baby, and the hotel sign in Lander, Wyoming, that invited us to "STAY HERE FOR THE REST OF YOUR LIFE." I found that ominous. I did not tell about the taxi in Saudi

Arabia, which I was not supposed to wait for *outside*. I created quite a stir in the hotel lobby by defying the concierge. Nor did I tell about the taxi in Manhattan that could not find New Jersey. I'll love that driver forever. He was from Bangladesh.

I wish you smooth roads, safe travels, decent drivers, and interesting conversations. These days, in a world of so many unanswerable questions, it is possible taxi drivers have developed and chiseled more good answers than the rest of us. Think of it—their audience time with passengers is so short. They have time to muse and to meditate, to sharpen and consolidate their perspectives. I still have not figured out how they find all the places they find.

Fabric Thrown over the City

HE SAYS, "YOU COULD CALL IT A SHAWL OR a scarf—I call it a fabric—but it's thrown over the city and only a few pinholes of light get through."

"Excuse me?" This is before a cup of coffee or anything. Six-thirty A.M. on a Saturday morning in New York City and the driver, staring up out his window, is pausing at a stoplight in a yellow taxi en route to Columbia University.

His voice is butter smooth and soft. "I think about the light, how it's always been there, when the

Indians were here and the old-time people and everything. And they thought their time was the real time and we think our time is the real time and no one's time is, really."

"Have you been up all night?" I say.

"No, why?"

"Just wondered."

He turns his head to the side and smiles. "I prefer morning to night. Do you?"

"Sure do. More energy."

I feel as if a certain mesmerizing fabric has been thrown over . . . our car.

There's hardly any traffic. The streets are ripe with that pre-buzz emptiness, pre-crowd, pre-everything. The streets feel like childhood, like our lives before things happen. There's so much that belongs to no one and to all of us, and mornings are rich enough to remember this.

The driver's damp blond hair rolls back in long waves. Odd how, with taxi drivers, you know the sides and backs of their heads. Somehow this feels very personal.

And he just keeps talking. "Occasionally the light seems like a strong, straight beam, and other times it's very faded and drifty. You know? There's a whole mood, the way light is. It's hard to know how a day will be when we first begin it. Like, we really don't know about today at all. Do we? We just hope. We have ideas. And we think we're wise, but we're not. We just want to be. The world is not your oyster. It is not mine, either. The world is not an oyster, period. The world is the world. Whoever said it was an oyster, do you know?"

"I do not."

"Why are you going out so early? Who are you going to see at Columbia? Smart people with big opinions?"

"Teachers at a conference."

"Oh. People you know or people you don't know?"

I have to think about it. Then I say, "After a while, everyone seems a tiny bit familiar, even if you've never met them before, don't you think?" His style is contagious.

He peers at me in the rearview mirror. "Do I seem familiar?"

"Yes, you do, sort of, but I don't know why exactly." I don't want to say James Dean. I have always missed James Dean in the world. I have caught him in shadings of a stance, a posture, an eyelid, a hand in a pocket, a tip of a head. I feel the same about Jack Kerouac. He died before I found his books. Then I started looking for him everywhere in the world. This taxi driver has James and Jack both, and he's not even standing up.

He says, "We are dreamers in a windy sky, see? Floating among buildings and schedules. All a dream. Like that 'Row Row the Boat' song. We're rowing right now, feel it? The whole world is rowing through the sky."

* * *

I stare out the window at pretzel carts and old men in faded raincoats and women with small sacks in their hands that might be a single bagel or a single muffin and ladies walking tiny nervous dogs on leashes. The stoplights click in predictable and comforting patterns. I think of that moment before a car starts up again after idling, how well we come to know that moment as passengers or drivers, either one. We are so accustomed to anticipation, being on the brink, pitching forward.

The driver never stops talking no matter what the car is doing.

He says, nodding his head slightly, "Today you will say things you can predict and other things you could never imagine this minute. Don't reject them, let them come through when they're ready, don't think you can plan it all out. This day will never, no matter how long you live, happen again. It is exquisitely singular. It will never again be exactly repeated—ouch! Did you see? That woman dropped her bag on the sidewalk and swooped it up again, did you see that? She will never again drop her bag in exactly the same spot. Don't ever forget it. Precious, precious, precious—oh. "

"I do know," I say to him, feeling a swoon overtaking me in rhythm with his words. "I know it and I care about it. Thoughts like that have occurred to me for a long time already, but I really like hearing you say them. I mean, it is so beautiful how you say them. I wish you were talking to these teachers today, not me. Seriously, and thank you."

We're driving past a park lined with overflowing trash cans. My driver sighs, staring through the wide-open window with his left arm dangling on the outside. He says, "Isn't it amazing how much garbage accumulates from one day to the next— just through the course of the hours? I wonder sometimes how cities hide dump sites so well. You'd think there would be more of them and we would see them everywhere, wouldn't you?"

"Yes."

Then he says, "Look, look up! Oh, how I love that. Early sun streaks. So beautiful. If you look up right now, the fabric cracked a little."

Way to Go

BUT HOW WILL I GET THERE? IT'S TOO FAR TO WALK.

Come on. Some people walk across the whole United States. They walk across Canada.

Peace Pilgrim walked back and forth across the United States many times. Did you ever hear of her? She wore a navy blue tunic and navy blue pants and simple navy tennis shoes, the old-fashioned kind. They didn't even have thick soles. She called no taxis, and carried no money, but her friends picked her up and drove her here and there within cities, then dropped her off at the city limits so she could walk from one town to the next. Peace Pilgrim refused to speak about her mysterious early life, and what had turned her into a pilgrim. Some people said she had been very rich, with a chauffeur, before she devoted her life to wandering around speaking about peace. She used to say, "I once had all the possessions one requires for a comfortable life—a car, a house, everything material—but it was not what I needed." *Live the way you believe, do meaningful work, find your own inner peace so you can work for world peace, speak in a true voice, you'll never be scared.*

My mother met her at a university when I was a baby, then stayed friends with her forever.

Peace Pilgrim would sleep in our house when she passed through town. She ate no meat and she never had colds. I stared at her so hard, as if I wanted to soak her up. College students came over to listen to her speak about peace in our living room. We drove her to radio stations for interviews.

She wouldn't tell her age. If someone asked, she would say, "I am *ageless*! We are all *ageless*!" She said it with an exclamation point.

Sometimes, when she had to, she slept in a cardboard box under an overpass. Snow fell, and she survived it by wrapping herself in paper. She believed in talking and listening to people even if they looked a little scary. If you found yourself lost, it was probably that other person sleeping under the bridge, the raggedy one in the rusty metal drum, who could tell you how to find your road again.

"But Mom," I used to say, after we'd dropped Peace Pilgrim at the side of the road again on a sunny autumn day, so she could walk to Kansas City, or Peoria, or Indianapolis. "What if she gets too tired to walk any farther? Won't she take a ride?"

"No," said my mother. "She'll just sleep wherever she is. She'll take a ride inside a city but between cities—walk, walk, walk."

I guess she was the first big traveler I knew, besides my dad. She marked me.

Mystery: Everything felt better before you got there than when you actually got there. When you actually got there, you didn't quite have the energy to be there.

Staring at the map, staring at the postcard picture of the motel with the kidney-shaped sky-blue swimming pool, felt much better than standing next to the dingy pool smelling the chlorine.

It was hard to wrap your mind around it.

Anticipation jingled and smelled like vanilla.

Arrival clunked. Huh? This is the place? This cluttered gift shop was worth stopping for? I don't think so. Let's get back on the road.

It took a while for the reality of being somewhere to replace the anticipation of being there.

Better standing back, just imagining.

* * *

It's too cold. It's too windy.

Someone will take you. Someone will pick you up.

What if they don't? What if I wave my hand, and no taxi stops?

Which hand do I wave? Is there a code? A method? And what does that light on top of the taxi mean? Empty or full? How do we learn all these things?

You'll put your life in the hands of people you don't know a million times. And it will be fine.

This is the human condition? Our lives in the hands of people we don't know?

This is the human condition. And trust me, you know everyone. You know them because you're human.

Shopping for Nothing

GRANDMA MARIE RODE A BUS FROM HER gloomy brick apartment with the shades drawn down to the heart of old St. Louis. She did this over and over. She felt less lonely in the world while riding a bus. She would have been too shy to ride in a taxi. It would have been expensive. No one in my family ever did anything expensive.

Also, a taxi might have required a conversation. Grandma Marie was expert at blending into a scene, repeating invisible phrases like "Never mind" and "Whatever you say."

Her husband dragged their laundry in a silver cart with wheels to a local OPEN 24 HOURS Laundromat at 3 A.M. so he could have the whole place to himself.

But she got lonely. She asked me if I wanted to ride downtown with her. Sometimes, if I didn't have school, I went along.

Bundled women stepped on and off the bus, nodding at one another from the aisle, black and white women mixed, women from the old European countries wearing fringed scarves, speaking in thick accents—"It's really a cold one, isn't it?"—and Grandma Marie belonged to the human race again. Sometimes a bus ride was all it took to feel better.

Coin dropped in a slot. The forward lurch of the wheels. We stopped near the zoo in Forest Park, but couldn't see the lions. We paused for a long time near the corner luncheonette. I could spy a long, gleaming counter studded with white plates and shiny napkin dispensers. I stared at the taxis lining up underneath our bus windows. I liked the sloped lights on their roofs, the big black lettering on the sides of their cars: CA6-6666. I wanted to call them.

Grandma Marie said she was going shopping but often came home with no parcel, no sack. When I went with her, she would stride up and down the St. Louis streets peering with great interest into the windows of stores. She appreciated the talent of window display artists—strings of beads, lavish glitter, folded-paper flower bouquets. She enjoyed the way skinny mannequins could be rearranged— hand on hip, one hand carrying a picnic basket or a beach umbrella. She repeated, "Oh my! Look at that." She put her hand on my shoulder, and we paused.

She often seemed timid to enter the stores. Then someone might ask her what she wanted. Grandma Marie was a soft gray flannel mouse clutching a pocketbook, poking her fluffy head out of her apartment hole. I could feel her shyness rubbing off on me. Sometimes she asked me to make an inquiry. "Go see what that big doll costs." She'd stand on the sidewalk while I ran inside to find a saleslady.

Other days we'd ride the elevators proudly, exploring sections of the stores that seemed arcane—men's sports, for example, or baby's shoes. Why did babies even need shoes?

In those days all the big department stores had tearoom restaurants. For lunch we ate dainty tuna sandwiches or stuffed peppers at a table for two. A lady wearing a frilled white apron pushed the desserts on a fancy decorated cart around the room. Everyone stopped talking to look at what she had. I picked the biggest pieces of cherry pie and lemon cake, of course. I picked chocolate éclairs and tapioca pudding.

My grandma and I felt secretly smart, watching the glittering ladies in the dining rooms. Lips on the edges of steaming cups of tea. All the lives that weren't ours. We could stare at them, which made them ours in a different way. If you held something inside your head—a delicious line of pearly buttons, a folded sweater, fancy perfume bottles on a shiny mirror on a counter, a silver bracelet on a wrist—it became yours, too. You couldn't lose it. My grandma owned the shopping bags, the feathered hats, and the salmon mousse on a platter. I owned the stoplights, the neon, the produce men in shirt-sleeves and white aprons outside the fish market, and all the lines of waiting, humming taxis.

Take Me with You

ROGER THE NEIGHBOR BOY ATTACHED A
small silver cart to his green bicycle and pulled me
around the neighborhood. He was thirteen; I was
three. He never talked to me any other time. We
left our houses without our parents. The wind blew
our hair high up from our heads. Roger wore a
green checkered shirt. He pedaled over the creek,
up the Harvey Hill, past the creepy old houses. He
pedaled past the farm where my mama bought
tomatoes and sweet potatoes. He said, "Which way
do you want to go?" and let me point the direction.

He turned where I said to turn. When we eventually circled back to the driveway between the pine trees that separated our houses, I did not want to get out of the little silver soup can with wheels. I sat firmly, holding onto the sides and staying very silent, and everyone laughed at me.

My father drove the blue Buick with three holes like nostrils in the side of the hood. One morning he ran off the road, only a few blocks from our house. Somehow he lost control of the car and coasted across a weedy ditch and into someone's driveway. I was in the front seat and hit my head on the dashboard. We didn't have seat belts in those days, but I didn't die. My mother thought I might have a broken nose. It was only bruised. My father felt terrible. He thought I would not trust his driving anymore after that, but I always did. Once when I was older, he stopped at a liquor store for me because I told him it sold dress patterns. That's what my friend Susie had told me, or so I thought.

I made my dad go inside and ask for an Empire pattern with a ribboned waist. I stayed in the car and watched all the men inside laughing at him through the big window.

My mother's friend Irma wore spectacles that fell down on her nose as she drove us around St. Louis in a large white car. Sometimes she popped them on top of her head. I wanted to give her a vision test. My brother and I kicked her seat from the rear. We acted bad. Her thick gray hair straggled free in large strands from a fat bun. She pumped the gas pedal in her car as if it were a pedal on a pump organ: *go, stop, jolt forward, sudden brake, crescendo.*

My brother and I felt dizzy. We would close our eyes, let our heads loll around on our shoulders, tell each other we were going to vomit all over her auto carpet. But then, after stopping at four boring places, Irma would roll into the frozen custard stall and we would order large cones of creamy vanilla and Irma and my mother would gulp root beer floats happily as little girls, islands of white floating on the fizzy brown, and all would be forgiven.

In second grade, gripped with stomachache, I took a taxi home by myself from school. My mother didn't have a driver's license or a car yet. An old jalopy driven by an elderly man managed to ram the taxi, right in front of our house. My mother, waiting nervously in the doorway for me to arrive, a few precious dollar bills clutched in her hand to pay the driver, saw this happen. She saw the driver's hat fly off his head into the backseat and she saw me bounce from one side of the seat to the other. Then I crawled up onto the ledge inside the back window to get a better look at the car that had hit us. I was fine. I was fascinated by having been in a wreck so innocently—in a stopped car in front of my own home. There was no telling what strange and unexpected things could happen in this world.

My mother, who was not at all happy that I had

needed to leave school in the first place, walked me to a lady doctor a few blocks from our house to see if I had a whiplash. This was shortly after the same doctor had checked my nose. The doctor said no. Children's necks were very *resilient*, she said.

School stress, stomachache, whiplash, resilience— was anything unrelated?

My mother drove us everywhere once she got a license. When I was nine, a policeman stopped us on Grand Avenue in St. Louis and gave her a ticket for speeding. She couldn't believe it. She thought she never sped. She cried bitterly and said she did not have the money to pay the ticket. I was in the backseat. We were parked next to one of those gigantic silos that held gas or water. I was terribly scared of silos because I thought they might blow up at any minute and could not believe the bad luck of being stopped by a policeman right next to one.

When I was twelve, playing second violin in a youth symphony, my mother's station wagon spun

out of control on an icy freeway, right after free-
ways were invented. She crossed the median and
the car lodged in a ditch on the other side. It was
terrifying. I tossed around the backseat with my
brother and my violin. No one was injured. The
violin stayed in tune. The man who drove the tow
truck stared at me standing back away from the
road in the snow with my violin case. "You wanna
play for me?" he said.

The concept of a getaway car always seemed alluring. When one was in a school classroom being
falsely accused of something, for instance—*BING!*
Press a button and your escape car would pull up
right outside the open window.

I loved roads we hadn't turned on yet, but knew
we would someday. O crumbling, mysterious back-
streets, nameless alleys, I prayed to you. Save me,
take me far away from the test we were always
building up to.

Being rich would be nice, so you could pay your traffic tickets and eat more frozen custard, but it wasn't as important as having a Big Life. To go farther than anyone could see from one set of streets, blocks, turn signals. To feel comfortable in different settings, even if you had never been there before— the other side of town, for example.

To have more than one point of gravity. To roll on and on and feel easy and hopeful, doing that.

In middle school, I wondered about what a person living this sort of life might be called: *Hobo. Wanderer. Nomad. Itinerant. Perpetual traveler. Vagrant.* I liked *vagabond* and *ragamuffin*, certainly no words anyone would write on the "personal goals" line of any application.

What would we need when we got anywhere?

Odd things. Not the things you thought. Fewer clothes, for example.

Always fewer clothes. Really only one other set of clothes—something warm and something cool, and underwear and pajamas. Maybe you should only pack your favorite clothes in a suitcase. I have always packed my bags for journeys deliberately but sometimes don't zip them up till it's time to leave. I keep taking things out.

I figured out early on I would definitely need a little bit of color, a piece of red-striped Mexican Indian cloth to place beside my bed, wherever I was. Even for a single night, it helped a new room feel like home.

I would need a decent bar of soap. I would always need a notebook and something to write with.

Dangerous Taxis

IN HIGH SCHOOL, WHEN I WAS IMMORTAL, invincible, and could not drive, I participated involuntarily in a number of car wrecks.

Amy, who would soon disappear from our school forever (some said she had gone off to a convent in a forest to have a mysterious baby), drove through a stop sign in downtown San Antonio and a gray station wagon crashed into us.

No one was hurt. We had to go to court, but I didn't have to pay anyone since I was just a passenger.

Tina, who drove with only one arm, encouraged

me to accompany her one night when she felt like borrowing our friend Bryan's car without permission from Bryan, to drive around the block. "Sure," I said. "Sounds great."

What was I thinking?

Tina crashed into the fancy mailbox of a dark brick bungalow. Somehow Bryan's car ended up atop the heap of bricks that had been supporting the mailbox. Two wheels were off the ground. Hard to do. Sort of like a circus act. The car was trapped, so to speak. We had to contact not only the police, but also a tow truck, and the people whose mailbox we had wrecked (actually, Tina had to use their telephone to make the calls, which must have been awkward—I stayed outside in the shadowy yard, whistling and worrying), and Bryan himself.

Tina did not have to contact her parents because they were dead, so we had to call mine.

Not one person in this story was happy.

My parents ordered me to stop riding in any car

they were not driving. But they were always at work. That meant I could walk, take the bus, ride a bicycle, or stay at the library for the next ten years. Although I had grown fond of riding the bus downtown to a little coffee shop named the Gate House, where waitresses in miniskirts served steaming cups of "Constant Comment" tea, there were many places the bus did not go. Or hours it did not go there. It was harder to coordinate one's life with a bus than many people who never ride one might imagine.

A year or so later, after attending a peace meeting held in the basement of a downtown music store, I stepped outside to feel windy gusts of cold sweeping the city. The season had changed while we were inside, summer to fall, boom. Texas is like that. I had no sweater. Suddenly I felt the awful scratch-and-sizzle-in-the-throat that foretold a coming cold. Shivering at the San Pedro bus stop, I decided it was the flu. I would definitely have to stay home from school the next day.

Moments later it felt like pneumonia.

Just then a burgundy Mustang with a large dent in the hood pulled up. The young man at the wheel rolled the window down on my side and leaned over to say, "You need a ride?"

My first thought was, I know him. He goes to my school; is he Billy Goodman's friend? I have just forgotten his name. Was he at that meeting?

"Sure do," I said. "Going north?"

He said, "Yep, hop in."

Within three blocks I figured out I did not know him. He had chains on his wrists and a rank, oily smell. His tight black tank top was streaked with grease. He jammed on the brakes too hard instead of slowing gradually. Worse was the way he looked at me. As if to say, "Aha! I've got her." I could see he was older than I'd thought, too. He veered into a gas station. "Stay right there," he said. He leaped from his seat, grabbed the nozzle, and began pumping gas into the car.

I took my cue, jumped out, and began running.

"What do you think you're doing?" he shouted after me.

"I'm home!" I yelled. "I live right here!"

A bus to anywhere was paused at the corner light. I ran to it, pounded on the door until it opened, and jumped on. The driver gave me a strange look. I threw some coins into the slot, not even noticing how many.

"Whoa! Whoa," said the driver. "Where are you going?"

"I am making a getaway," I gasped. "Something terrible was just about to happen. You saved me." I sank down in my seat and could not bear to look out the window, to see if the oily man was chasing us. The driver kept turning his head to stare at me.

This was only one of the many things I never told my parents.

A few years later I was riding around with a

young man when he said, "Let's take off our clothes and drive to Austin."

"Why?" I said.

"It would be fun. I know some people who did it and they said it was a lot of fun."

"What was fun about it?" I asked. "I don't think it sounds like a good idea at all."

"People in other cars looked over at them. They tried to see if they were really naked all the way down."

"And that was fun?"

He stared at me. We were not destined to be friends for long, that was certain. We were not on the same highway, brother. We were not on the same *map*.

My friend Beth and I hitchhiked in Wisconsin together and accepted a ride in a dump truck. We were on our way to see my grandfather, who was dying, in a little town where he had *no history at all*. A solemn German Lutheran, and a hoarder of old newspapers, he did not want to die in St. Louis, where he and Grandma Marie had lived most of their lives. I kept thinking of my poor Grandma after he hauled her up north a few years earlier. She was now conscripted to a tiny town that had no department stores or tea carts or shop windows. I could not blame her for descending into a stubborn silence for many months before she died.

Beth and I had ridden a Greyhound bus from Texas to Wisconsin. We were encamped at my aunt's tourist cabins on a glistening lake outside Eagle River, working as her maids and looking for a summer adventure. I would snap out the fresh sheets and Beth would grab the other ends. We wrapped the lumpy mattresses for the next unsuspecting guests who did not realize that my aunt, the owner of the cabins, was extremely difficult.

"Why are you up here?" asked the truck driver, who seemed slightly grumpy but not dangerous.

"We are here because my grandfather is dying

here," I said. "We are working as maids for my aunt, who lost nine babies and has become very bitter. We may have made a mistake to come."

"Nine babies?" he said. "That is terrible. Miscarriages?"

"Some were miscarriages. Others actually got born and died soon after birth."

"That's very sad. But why do you hitchhike?"

"We don't have a car. We don't even have driver's licenses."

"Why doesn't your aunt drive you?" We were passing signs for Wisconsin dairy products, with large wedges of yellow cheese painted on them.

"She is too bitter. We would also rather ride with someone we don't know than someone who drinks beer after breakfast."

He eyed us carefully. Maybe he thought we were just big complainers.

"I wouldn't hitchhike if I were you," he said in a serious tone. "If I had a daughter your age, I would not want her to hitchhike. Please take my advice. Don't do this again."

"Are you going to beat us up?" asked Beth. We were passing between two deep forests right then. I shuddered.

"No, I am not," he said. "But someone else might. I know the world of truckers better than you do, and I advise you to get driver's licenses or take a taxi whenever you can."

I said, "Are there taxis out here?"

Later Beth would always say, "Remember when I asked the truck driver if he was going to beat us up?"

And I would always say, "Stop it, Beth."

Shortly after we were back in Texas, my grandfather died. A few years later my aunt startled everyone by having a stroke and dying, too. She was very young to die. I would regret that my last word to her, when she called us lazy losers for quitting after ten days, had been "Bitch!" I had never said that word out loud before, and it seems awfully shameful now. How strange to believe in peace on a world level and not be able to get along with members of your own family.

I would think of the truck driver and his advice about taxis and how I never hitchhiked again and the way he stared at me when I said, "Nine babies" and how it had been so easy to tell someone I never saw before another person's deep life tragedy. Maybe that was wrong to do. On a train to Oklahoma once, a young man named Leo sitting in the seat in front of me told me he was running away from his own wedding. He showed me the rings.

Taxi,
North from Jerusalem

THE ARAB DRIVER THREATENED TO STOP
because my friend and I were kissing madly in his
backseat. You just did not do that in the Middle
East. It was unthinkable, sensational, rude.

"I stop here, yes! You get out. You walk!"

He peered into his rearview mirror at us and we
did not care.

We pretended we did not speak English or
Arabic.

We spoke only the language of kissing in that
land of love and faith and fighting.

Kissing was addictive. Once you started . . .

He drove slowly but he did not stop.

My family lived eight miles north of the walled city, out in the rough countryside.

I have no memory of why my friend was in the taxi with me. He lived downtown in Jerusalem, inside the wall. We had been to a concert or a film. Bus service stopped at sundown. You had to take a taxi if no one was picking you up. My friend would have had to take a return taxi trip home without me. Maybe he was being a gentleman.

My father thought no boys were gentlemen. He would have been horrified and furious to know I was kissing anyone in a semipublic place, in his conservative homeland, witnessed by a driver who could spread the word among all the other drivers: "That girl kisses." It must have been awkward for the driver, who was no doubt a distant cousin of my father, since everyone who walked the Jerusalem streets was a distant cousin of everyone else back then. The seat was cool—folds of black leather, rounded seams. The taxi, with windows wide open, rolled between the dark meadows and hillsides of old Palestine, studded with the mounded bodies of slumbering sheep among the stones. We were living a single year there that would change our lives forever.

I was kissing someone I would see again ten years later on the other side of the earth. Then I would say to him, "You talk too much. You chatter. Man oh man, could you ever be quiet for at least sixty seconds?"

He would say, "What do you mean, 'chatter'?"

How cruel. I am, perhaps, the biggest chatterbox on earth.

We would stand in the fading light between nearly dead trees in the state of Tennessee and I would say, "No, I don't think I can marry you after all. I need more silence in my days," and he would say, "Okay then." We would ride a swinging cable car to the top of a mountain, stand apart from each other, and never kiss once. We would look down on three states and say, "Okay, it's over."

Not one more word would ever pass between us.

In the years that followed I have thought of the uncomfortable taxi driver more than the person I kissed in his car.

What Happens

You open your hand. You reach out for something. *I want, I want, give it to me.* First the soft rabbit, the shiny spoon. The bath toy. You open your hand to the world and expect the world to put something back in it.

Transaction.

Once the transactions begin, the baby gets interesting.

In school a raised hand means you have a question, or *you know.* Sometimes the arm is very heavy. It is hard to raise up, but something tells you your life will be worse if you don't. *I'll take a guess.*

Years later, on a city street, you lift your arm, freeze your fingers at a certain imploring angle or wave them back and forth and expect something to stop for you. Pick you up. Drive you. Drop you off.

Sometimes there is a meter. You try not to watch it. Watching makes the numbers increase more quickly. You try to notice the scene outside the window. Cardboard boxes being unloaded in front of delicatessens. A large sack of fresh clams on top of a pile of groceries on a rolling dolly. Sunlight is falling onto the clams. "Get those clams into a refrigerator quickly," you want to call out the window. But they are not your clams and you are gone, gone, gone.

Sometimes there is a set price. Sometimes, especially in other countries, you can't understand what the price is going to be and you still take the taxi, worried for the whole ride. Then at the other end there is some negotiating to deal with. Sometimes it is easy.

Many times you get a bonus. A taxi driver tells you one wondrous thing during the journey. It rings in your ears all day.

An impeccably neat driver from Ghana in Washington, D.C., told me he could solve all the government's problems in two weeks, if given the chance. But no one had asked for his advice yet.

A late night driver in Pittsburgh said, "I dream about staircases under the bed going down to other worlds. Do you?"

"No," I said. "But it sounds interesting."

"Do you think I should write about it? Make it be a story or something?" he said.

"You bet. I think people should write about everything."

Before I stepped out of his car, he said, "Do you know the secret to success?"

"No," I said, thinking it might be a joke or something.

He said solemnly, "Oh, I thought you might. You don't really seem like a regular person."

An African-American driver in D.C. whose dad was a lawyer said he misses the old days when you could tell a person's profession by what he or she carried. "Like, housepainters carried ladders. Lawyers carried briefcases. Now everyone carries briefcases. Chimney sweeps carried those big ol' brooms."

"Chimney sweeps? You used to see them?"

"Hell, yes. I loved them. They were everywhere."

On the Isle of Mull, Scotland, a driver let us out near a boat dock. He pointed to a boat that had a sign on the side of it: THIS IS NOT THE ULVA FERRY. "That's your boat," he said. We were going to the Isle of Staffa, to see flocks of puffins. No people live on Staffa. The driver said, "Aye, then, you'll have a bonnie wee walk over there among the birdies. Puffins let you get very close up. Since they don't know about people, they're not afraid of us." We'd passed the Dervaig Church on the way to the dock and he said, "There's a bonnie wee church." He told us not to pet any seal pups if we saw them sunning. "They have very sharp teeth." He said he liked Mull because there were so many places where, "even on a beautiful day, you never see more than one person."

In New Orleans I stayed at a hotel with tiny towels and a trick shower, but I loved that city so much it didn't matter. On my way to the airport I said to the taxi driver, "Gee this is a wonderful place. Everything is delicious—food, music, architecture. . . . I guess most people feel that way."

He nodded his tall head without speaking, but I could see him smiling in the mirror.

"Where you from, miss?"

"Texas."

"Most Texans like Louisiana, yes," he said, nodding more.

We were passing a cemetery with elaborate white monuments like miniature castles.

I said, "And do most Louisianans like Texas?"

He looked to one side, spoke softly. "Not a lot."

Taxis lined up glistening in rain outside Heathrow.

Rounded, old-fashioned black sedans.

Suddenly we're driving between cobblestone walks and houses with flowerpot chimneys. Radio tuned to British accent news. Driver chatting about traffic toward Suffolk County.

Astonishing how planes just deposit us in different countries and the taxis wait to pick us up! I will never take it for granted. It is a central miracle of existence, right up there next to breathing.

Taxis in Jordan late at night would stop no matter what word we called out. They could see in the dark. Swooping up and down the steep hills of Amman, they pulled up neatly to curbs without even screeching.

I did experiments. I called out, "Hope! Pain!" in English, and they stopped just as surely as if I had said, "Taxi!"

"Yes, madam, where you like to be going?" Bowling alley? All-night café?

One taxi driver in Jordan said, "I really like books of Mark Twain, you ever read Mark Twain?"

Sometimes your driver is so bad you have to leap out.

Coleman and I jumped out once in New York City when our driver from Afghanistan, shouting angrily into a telephone, was nipping curbs, swerving, and slamming on brakes at random moments in the crowded streets. He steered in such a jolting, haphazard manner that we threw money at him and escaped at a stoplight, dragging our book bags. I grabbed a light pole for balance. Coleman stood on the pavement, breathing deeply. "Oh man," he said, "I could tell it was going to get worse."

The minute I got into a taxi in Philadelphia, the driver said, "I love *Star Trek*, do you?"

"Not at all," I said. "But once I attended a *Star Trek* convention and our son won second prize in the costume contest."

"Fantastic. Who was he?"

"Data. The pale guy?"

"You bet. So your boy likes it?"

"Loves it. So does my husband."

"But you never watch with them?"

"Never once."

He paused for a second, shaking his head.

Then he launched into his selected auto-biography.

"Well, when my best friend got killed a few years ago, I turned to the *Tibetan Book of the Dead* for comfort. Have you ever read it? It really helps. I have it on a tape here in my car. If we were going farther, I'd play it. My dreams are much clearer when I don't eat meat. Yours, too? I went to a

health food store a few months ago and bought bottled water and soybeans. After eating them for a
few days, my dreams grew the clearest ever. When
I ate a pork chop later, I threw up. Of course life
can't end. Don't you agree? It must go on in cycles.
Reincarnation is the most obvious thing in the
world. Check out those trees. They're dead as hell,
then they're alive again. Recently my wife was
stomping on ants in our kitchen and I asked her to
consider all the backs she'd broken and families
she'd disrupted. She called me a piss-ant and told
me to shut up. But I meant it. "

When he dropped me off, I honestly could not
remember where I was, or why I was going there.
My head felt like a speed dial. I liked it. And usually I only like going slow.

At the book signing after my reading, a woman in
a gray winter coat said, "Please sign this book for
my cat. He really likes your poetry. His name is Ed.
E-D for Ed. "

I stared at her hard and she wasn't smiling.

So I signed the book, "To Ed, Happy poetry and purring! Love, Hamilton."

She snatched the book away from me and stared at it. "Who is Hamilton?"

"*My* cat."

She slammed the book back down on the table. "No! He doesn't want your cat's name, he wants yours. Sign it again!"

So I crossed out Hamilton and wrote my own name, tentatively. My script had a shaky look.

Then she slapped an aging chocolate chip cookie on the table and said, "Eat it! Ed sent it to you!"

I popped it in my pocket and thanked her, oh my Friskies, you bet I did. I said I'd eat it later.

How much I wished the same *Star Trek* taxi guy would pick me up again afterward so I could tell him this. But I got a silent guy listening to a ball game.

The Thread

IT IS IMPOSSIBLE TO FOLLOW THE THREAD IN advance of things happening. You can only detect it later, trailing out behind you.

If Dubby had not guided me to my first class on the first day of college, he might never have suffered his beloved white GTO being smashed up against a telephone pole, thanks to my calico cat that needed a ride.

Dubby and the cat had one thing in common, besides the accident. They both went by initials, not names.

The cat was DC and Dubby was, legally, W.I. I had imagined that DC, attached to the cat when it came to us, meant Dear Cat, but no one ever confirmed this. Surely it did not mean the capital city of our land. Dubby's mom, who had five sons, had given her youngest the initials W.I. as a designation at birth, in memory of his grandfather, Washington Irving Davis, who was always called "Mr. W.I." As he grew, people called him Dubby—later still he would shorten it to "Dub."

And what does GTO stand for? I still don't know. It was a car. It was a popular car.

Eventually it stood for: Good-bye To Our Outings.

On my first day of college my father had dropped me off by the school fountain and said, "Good luck." I would be living with my parents and brother at home a few miles away from campus instead of in a dorm. College seemed overwhelming.

Dubby looked so confident and friendly when I

met him on the steps of the campus bookstore. He had thick, bright red hair hanging straight to his shoulders. He stood out. I hadn't even seen his car yet. I asked for directions. He pointed me toward a building where my first class was located. He was a sophomore. He knew things.

The first class went okay. It was English. English always felt like a friendly universe. Books to read, papers to write. I could do that.

The next class, psychology, had sixty people in it and focused on the behavioral patterns of rats. We would test their feeding patterns with tiny food pellets and Skinner boxes, small "laboratory conditioning chambers" with levers. We would conduct friendly noninvasive experiments, keeping charts, writing up our results. I forget what this was supposed to demonstrate. Having raised rats for a few years in high school as a private hobby, I felt pretty confident about this, too. But statistics had never before been involved.

When the teacher, a small, edgy man who resembled my old favorite white rat Ralph, assigned us partners for the entire semester, my partner turned out to be Dubby. I couldn't believe it since he was practically the only person on the campus I'd spoken to so far. Dubby turned around in his chair and waved at me.

We were fairly vigilant about our rat feeding for the first few months, then things started falling apart. I developed bronchitis with a high fever and had to stay home for a whole week. The doctor was mad at me for being a vegetarian. He said I was anemic and had to eat meat if I wanted to get well. My mother made me chicken soup. I hated it. I dreamed of lamb chops weeping on a plate. I dreamed of eating rats. I tossed and turned in my sweaty bed.

Dubby, on his own with our experiment, forgot to keep the chart up-to-date. I kept phoning to remind him, but he was never at home. Dubby was an extremely talented guitarist and singer. He told me his band practiced a lot. When I caught up with him by phone one midnight, he said, "Oh God. I forgot." We would not be able to tally our final rat results if sections of our chart were empty.

At midterm our professor posted a list of students who weren't doing so well and we were on it. Dubby wasn't worried. I was horrified. I pressed my face to the rat cage, begging our boys to work overtime.

I had failed my third test for a driver's license— once I hit the rubber cones between lanes, once I bashed into the curb while parallel parking, once I argued with the driving teacher who told me to turn left after urging me into the right lane. Was this a trick? The Texas Department of Public Safety said I had to wait three months before attempting to get a license again. So I was Dubby's frequent passenger, but he was nice about it. If you were proud of your car, you didn't mind driving people around.

Dubby's GTO was sleek and white, with a roaring loud engine, stock 389 cubic inches, and triple-barrel carburetors with progressive linkage. If you didn't press the accelerator too hard, only one of the carburetors kicked in. So you could save gas. I didn't know what the hell he was talking about, but I accumulated a lot of information.

We listened to Elton John at top volume on his Craig cassette deck through six-inch Pioneer padded speakers in each front door. We had just passed through the pitiful eight-track tape era which lasted approximately four months, long enough for college students to waste a lot of money on fat music tapes we were never going to be able to play again. But Dubby believed in technology. He said his car had "once been compared to the Hoover Dam."

Dubby drove me to hear his fabulous band play at a nearby military canteen. All the soldiers in the canteen got up and danced. I could see that rats were not going to figure prominently into Dubby's future. He wasn't a scientist. One of his bandmates would later become a major star—Christopher Cross. I would be a young married person shopping at a neighborhood grocery store years later and hear Chris Cross, not quite his real name, singing "Sailing" over the loudspeakers. Dubby would play and sing all over the place for decades. He's still doing it, and now his incredibly talented daughter sings with him sometimes. Who can ever guess what happens next?

Back then, we were sailing through our days. Such sweet sailing, and we never even knew it. It felt hard. My cat DC, months overdue on his rabies shot, was living mostly outdoors in the suburban wild, with squirrels and free rats and possums. DC needed to go to the vet, but my mom and dad always seemed to be working during the daytime when the vet's office was open. It would have been impossible to take DC on a bus.

Although Dubby was a dog person himself, he said he would be happy to drive the cat and me to the vet in the GTO. He didn't blink. He didn't feel his life with his beloved car coming to a swift and unexpected close.

I had no cat carrying case in those days. I just hoisted the gigantic rumpled calico in my arms till we got into the car, and then the irritated cat immediately dove under the front seat. Dubby said, "I have a big surprise for you." He popped James Taylor's brand-new album, *Mud Slide Slim and the Blue Horizon*, into the tape deck. I was a James Taylor fanatic. James and I shared the same birthday, along with Jack Kerouac, coincidences which made me feel upbeat about my own existence.

Dubby said, "I just hope that cat isn't going to seize my ankles. Tell me it doesn't do that."

I said, "I don't know what it does. We don't usually drive around."

Dubby and I sped north on Nacogdoches,

grooving to James, drinking in the sunlight, feeling good about the earth.

At the veterinary clinic I was able to drag the cat out from under the passenger seat, though he dug his claws into the carpet and yowled. He hid his furry face in the crook of my arm while receiving his injection. Dubby had stayed outside in the parking lot. He was polishing his lights or something.

It was while we were on the way home that a wild shopper swerved out from a mall parking lot and smashed Dubby's gleaming GTO up against a telephone pole. The shopper hit us right in the center on the driver's side. We weren't hurt, but we were shocked.

When the policemen arrived, they helped us out of our crumpled seats and kept repeating, "Are you hurt? Move your head, move your arms." I kept saying, "There's a cat under the seat. Don't let him run away!"

The policemen said, "Does he bite?"

"Yes!" I said. "Especially when he's panic-stricken."

Dubby stood nearby with his hands in his pockets, staring at the bashed-in car. We were lucky not to be injured. He popped his James Taylor tape out of the deck. He didn't look mad or stunned. He looked composed. I think he even whistled something. Dubby's crumpled GTO looked brilliant in the sunlight. The other driver, frenzied and disoriented, kept declaring he hadn't seen us. I stared at him, thinking, You're drunk with shopping, sir.

DC was disgusted by this whole experience. He stayed underneath the seat. He sank his claws into the carpet and refused to be dragged out, till right before the tow truck hauled the car away. I thought, Maybe he will die of shock, after getting his shots and all. Too much stress for one day.

I can't remember how we got home. Who drove us? A policeman? I kept apologizing madly to Dubby, "I feel so terrible about your car!" He would never drive it again. It was nice of him not to blame me.

Shortly after that my mother ran over DC in the driveway and he died on the spot. Shots up-to-date but cat: dead.

We got Cs in the rat class.

Dora

A VERY OLD WOMAN I'D NEVER SEEN BEFORE was sitting in the backseat of my car when I came out of the pharmacy. I had only been away from the vehicle a few moments, but had forgotten to lock it. I opened the door and stared at her. "May I help you?" I said. So far having a driver's license had been more of a problem than a pleasure.

She wore a flowered pink dress and a white sweater. Her hands were folded in her lap and a small white plastic pocketbook sat next to her on the seat. She was sitting in the middle, over the hump. She didn't answer.

"Excuse me? I think you may have the wrong car?"

No reply. She cast her eyes toward the carpet.

I waved my hand, urging her out. She didn't budge. Nothing. I looked around the parking lot. There was no one to help me.

The previous week I had placed a friend's borrowed violin bow on the roof of the car while unlocking the door. My friend had said I could use his bow for one night only, since my own needed new horsehair. I had driven off with the bow on the roof. Fifteen minutes later, realizing what I had done, I made a wild U-turn. The bow was splintered into sad scraps of wood and horsehair in the middle of McCullough Road. I had to pay my horrified friend more than a hundred dollars.

Now I had a passenger. She didn't seem like a robber, and I was already broke, but what to do with her?

"Please? *¿Por favor?*"

She wouldn't look at me.

This situation had not been included in the dull driving manual I had been poring over, reluctantly, for more than a year. So far every problem I had encountered in my life had not been predicted or described by anyone in advance. No one had told me my shoe would fly off into the audience in elementary school when I sang a solo on the stage. No one had suggested a donkey might stomp me to the ground at Girl Scout camp. I had never imagined I could get a concussion from a soap dish in a hotel shower.

"*¿Cómo se llama?*" I asked the lady, trying to smile.

"Dora." She didn't smile back.

"*Bueno*, Dora, *adios!*" I waved her out of the seat again.

She looked down at her lap as if I were hurting her feelings.

So I took her home to my parents, whom I still lived with. I took her back to our humble brick house with its loquat tree and patch of mint.

I talked all the way there, mixing English and Spanish, hoping my chatter might cause a clue to burst from her lips. We drove onto our street called Arroya Vista. The vista had deteriorated considerably when a car wash recently replaced the vacant green field at the corner. I pulled into the driveway and opened Dora's door again, but she wouldn't get out. I closed the door.

I ran into the kitchen where my father was drinking Arabic coffee from a small cup and frowning. Since he worked for the newspaper, he always frowned when he read it. Grammatical errors made him go wacko.

"Dad," I said. "There's a lady in the car and I can't get her out." It sounded so weird.

He looked at me sadly. "Didn't I tell you never to pick anyone up?"

"I didn't, Dad. She got into the car when I was in the drugstore. She seems shy and confused. She is also ancient."

"Take her to the police station," he said.

"No!" said my mother, who had entered the room. "If she's shy, that will scare her." My mother raised one finger. "Never scare the elderly," she said.

"Yeah," I said. "But I'm a little scared myself."

"Go with her, Miriam," my father said to my mother. "Take her to the newspaper. Let someone there interview her."

My mom pulled long pants over her yoga tights and carried a small glass of lemonade out to Dora.

Dora drank it.

My mom didn't speak any Spanish, so she talked in her high-up chicken voice, which she thought was understood by speakers of every tongue.

"Where do you live, Dora?" (Cheep cheep!)

"Dora, could we make a telephone call for you?" (Cheep cheep?)

Even chickens couldn't understand her.

Dora didn't utter a word.

My mom climbed into the backseat next to Dora and said to me, "Drive!"

She was trying to make Dora feel comfortable by sitting right beside her. She patted Dora's hands.

"Just drive slowly and I'll watch her face. Let's see if I can get a clue." She also sniffed, "That's ridiculous, what your father said about taking her to the newspaper. What a far-fetched idea."

I drove south on Blanco Road, where nothing was really white. I drove by the funky red-rimmed tortilleria, the pink beauty school where you got high on hair spray the minute you entered the door, and the green auto body shop. I drove past the street where old Bill Ward, master violin repairman, lived. I drove past the bloody meat market and the cut-rate shoe store, and all the streets named by homesick Californians. I turned left on Fresno. It was very strange to drive around without a destination.

My mother peeped and clucked in the backseat. She reported that Dora was looking drowsy. She tried to ask her (emphatic hand-to-mouth movements) if she might be hungry. No response. I asked her in Spanish. *Nada.*

Lemony light fell onto my hands on the steering wheel. Already I felt homesick for a life in which I was the driven, never the driver myself. Maybe driving was too much responsibility. I said, "Mom, what are we going to do? Maybe the newspaper *isn't* such a bad idea. Or should we go to the Mission Drive-in movie when it gets dark? Dora could be our zombie date."

"STOP!" my mother shouted. "She smiled!"

I veered into a used car lot, where a salesman began walking toward us with interest. I waved him away. The last thing I needed was *another* car.

Turning my head, I saw Dora smiling and pointing perkily at a street sign right behind us. And what did it say? What did it (cheep! cheep!) say?

It said, "DORA."

She had told me her street, not her name.

I just didn't understand.

We drove slowly down Dora Street with a happy woman whose name we would never know, till she pointed at a small yellow house with a crooked porch and a pot of red geraniums. She leaned forward, put her hand on my arm, and squeezed it hard before disembarking, muttering to herself.

My mother jumped out of the car, too, gazing fondly from the sidewalk to make sure our friend had a key to her own door. Then she slid into the front passenger seat and said, "What fun!"

Random Taxis

PALMER HOUSE HOTEL, CHICAGO, EST. 1871.

Newspaper accounts in 1924 about the lavish hotel stated: "A twenty-one year old guest taking a Saturday night bath in a different tub each week would be sixty-four years old before he had reclined in the last of the tubs. And a restless guest who insisted on changing his room every morning would be six years older before receiving his bill."

The first elevators in the hotel were called a "per-pendicular railroad."

When I read this kind of information, I feel well

fed. Perhaps this means I am digesting facts. I could stand off to the side of the fancy lobby and think about these things all day. Recently my mother asked me, "How full is your head?"

Small, tight yellow roses in round glass bowls with three little feet each are displayed on the check-in desk. Some white baby's breath tucked in between the roses. This will be the floral display I try to replicate when I get home.

Today the rain is pounding down and no one seems excited about reading Palmer House history. They are only excited about Not Getting Wet. For the ten steps between the taxi and the hotel door, they struggle with umbrellas. Many umbrellas whip inside out immediately. That's Chicago for you. I am standing in the anteroom between the World Outside and the lobby, reading hotel history, admiring the wet and gleaming taxis, dreaming of dinner.

When I see the rules in taxicabs, or the little

black-and-white mug shots of drivers on the visors, with their names attached and the dates of their licensing, something lights up. When I hear the taxi radios tuned to a certain station and it is never the station I would have listened to myself, never once, I feel a shimmering sense of the Wider World. It's right there, so close, but it may remain as secretly contained as the engine of the car, the valves and belts, unless you are

lucky.

A taxi driver in Dallas says ten people control the universe. They are the ones in charge of the plastic, the credit cards, behind the scenes, under the tables. "Trust me," he says.

I ask an African-American driver in North Carolina about his favorite places. He says, "I have never been out of North Carolina in my life. No, that's wrong, I've been to the beach of South Carolina. But it doesn't really count as a different state in my opinion because it's still a Carolina.

Basically I think the Carolinas are all I'm ever going to need."

He says he likes names. "Tell me your full name very slowly," he says. "Middle name, too."

I say, "It's my maiden name, not really middle," and spell "Shihab." He is silent when I say it is Arabic.

Then he says, "In North Carolina our friendliness is trueness. Like when we say 'How are you?' we really want to know. It's not just talk."

Then he says, "Basically it's just empty talk that might kill us all. Did you read where the president said every war looks good on paper?"

I say, "Not only did I read it, I went crazy when I read it. I wrote about it at length in my notebook."

He says, "Sir, a war never looks good. Not on paper, not on toilet paper, especially not on bandages soaked in blood. It does not look good at all. Even the churchy people regret voting for war now."

Greenhouse

I ONLY LOVED ONE CAR IN MY LIFE AND IT WAS
the first one I drove, the one I bought from my parents shortly after I got my license, a cream-colored
Mercedes Benz, circa 1965. It had a sunroof and a
sense of deep gravity—even the closing thud of the
doors was serious. My parents bought the Mercedes
for not very much money in Germany in 1967, after
our family's harum-scarum year in Jerusalem. We
brought it to the United States on the *Queen Mary,*
on the ship's second-to-last ocean crossing.

How exotic I felt, standing on the dock in view of

the Statue of Liberty, watching our car be unloaded. Then we drove it to Texas and started our new life. Later my dad sold the Mercedes to me for even less money. The car didn't have a radio, so I installed one. The strangest part was the license plate, which was *not* a vanity plate, but people thought it was— EGG-65. The car had yellow seats, too, like an egg.

I drove that car all over Texas, for many years, till it broke down and I learned the terrible phrase "The block is cracked."

"Well, what the hell is the block?" I asked the car repairman.

He said, "More money than you want to know about."

I won't go into the details, but my beloved first car ended up in a field in south Texas with giant sunflowers growing inside it—fat yellow petals sticking out through the sunroof. I imagine it has nearly gone back to soil by now. Once I took the poet W. S. Merwin and his wife, Paula, to see my old car, after it had been in the field more than ten years. We were on a tour of Texas wonders—from Big Bend National Park to the Santa Ana Wildlife Refuge to EGG-65. William said, "Have you written about it?" and I said, "I can't. It's really too painful. I made some bad choices and my car became a greenhouse."

All the cars since then have been lesser in nature—worthy of friendship but never true love. Lynxes, Sentras, Foresters—compared to EGG-65 they are dim bulbs, bereft of magic and elegance and that rich Mercedes hum.

Passport

A RICKSHAW DRIVER IN AGRA, INDIA, ON NEW Year's Eve did not want to take us to the Taj Mahal. "We go to rug store now, you look at rugs, you happy, you see Taj later in day, at twilight, more pretty if you see later."

"We no want rug shop. We traveling with backpacks. We no carry rugs for next three months."

"Listen lady, you can be shipping rugs. Very easy, shopkeeper will ship rugs for you no problem. Rugs waiting when you get home."

"No. No rugs. Taj or nothing. Let us out."

He pedaled us to the Taj, reluctantly. Large pink pom-poms on braided strings swung back and forth from his handlebars. We entered the magical monument we had seen in so many pictures and walked around it in silence. People always say, "You cannot believe how beautiful the Taj Mahal really is until you are standing inside it." They are right. We did not take any pictures of our own.

When we stepped back into the street, our same rickshaw taxi jingled its bells. The petulant driver had waited for us. Something felt even more ruined in the clutter and chaos of the city after standing in the majestic, silent Taj Mahal.

We asked to get out of the rickshaw at a Chinese restaurant. The driver tried to charge us a lot because he had waited for us. We said, "We did not ask you to wait." He said, "But you are happy I did, yes?" We gave him a little extra but refused to pay the large amount he was asking for.

We ordered vegetarian fried rice.

My love and I ended up arguing with each other, on the brink of a new year. I said, "You want to take the second-class train to Jaisalmer tomorrow? Feel free. Take it by yourself. I'm sure it will be as fantastic as that taxi was. I'm taking first class. See you at the other end."

He said, "Second class would be more interesting."

I said, "That's an interesting I can live without. It's a twenty-hour train ride, for God's sake. You want to be second class for twenty hours? Be my guest. Those days are behind me. I rode in the back of a truck with you and some cows on our honeymoon in Peru. Forget it. First class is like what, only a few rupees more? That's nothing! Are you nuts? In second class you sit upright on hard benches pressed together. In first class you might have a horrible little bunk, but at least there aren't a hundred other people in your compartment."

He kept staring at me silently over our pitiful chipped cups of tea. I could have continued yammering till the year changed, so finally he said, "Okay, we'll both take first class." He didn't look like he liked me very much.

The next day, unbelievably, the same fussy rickshaw driver was parked at the curb outside our humble hotel. He began jingling the bells the minute we stepped outside. "You going train station now, I take you."

My love said to me, "Did you ask him to come?"

"Of course not," I snapped.

First class on the train was dusty and disgusting. What a letdown.

It was also freezing cold, so we wrapped ourselves in layers of clothes. My love would hardly speak to me. I kept saying things like, "Maybe it *would* be warmer down in second class, all pressed together, why don't you go see?" The train conductor narrowed his eyes and said he would loan me a blanket if I gave him my pen. But it was my only pen. I talked him into taking a little money for a blanket instead. Then he asked me for candy. I didn't have any candy.

The rickshaw taxi of Agra looked better once we had seen the train.

In Paris we had a great time one Valentine's week—hiked by the Seine, ate croissants and crispy fish—but my pardner left his favorite hat in the taxi that took us to the airport. Miraculously, the taxi driver, with a Parisian care for detail, drove it back to the hotel. Weeks later the grimy brown hat arrived by post.

I now think of it as the hat that stayed in France longer than we did.

Taxi riding in Mexico became a scary enterprise. If you went to Mexico, everyone said, "Don't take a Volkswagen Bug. No bugs. Sorry, sorry! Scary bugs. Abduction taxis. Ring of thieves. Steer clear."

Many people were being kidnapped by VW bug

taxis. I have no idea where they were taken or if they ever came back. One Mexican friend told me every family she knew in Mexico City included at least one person who had been robbed by a taxi driver.

What about all the honest taxi drivers of Mexico?

I felt sorry for them. Walking around the city, a traveler was forced to repeat over and over again, "No, I don't need a ride! I'll walk! I love to walk!"

Teenagers hopped through the plaza on pogo sticks. They rolled down boulevards on kick scooters and mini-motorbikes.

One day you realize you're someone else's driver and you'd better get used to it—for months, years, whatever. Our son was two when we came over the ridge of the highway from which you can see the downtown buildings, the neighborhood in which we live, and he pointed and said, "Home!"

Happiness rippled through me. He was strapped

into his blue car seat, wearing his little red shoes with buckles.

For some reason I started singing "Somewhere over the Rainbow" very loudly. He did not know this song yet, but he listened. I felt the power of the driver surging within me—you pick the speed, you turn the air conditioner or radio on or off, you sing as loudly as you want, to your captive audience.

The Same Bed

A DRIVER PICKED ME UP AT A HISTORIC BED and breakfast inn in South Bend to take me to the airport in Chicago.

He said, "Let me guess—you were visiting Notre Dame."

"Wrong."

"You are thinking of moving here and came for an interview."

"Nope."

"What were you doing?"

"Well, uh, last night I was really tired, but I just

couldn't sleep. I lay awake all night. Does that ever happen to you?"

"Never. Did you take a sleeping pill?"

"No. I read the entire guest book in my room."

"And what did it say?"

"Well, one father had just married off his precious daughter Camille and had deeply mixed feelings about it. One couple was celebrating their fifth anniversary, but suffering serious problems in their marriage. One couple had just left their son at college and felt proud but very sad. And another couple on their wedding night reported they got spider bites in the bed where I was trying to sleep."

"And you wonder why you couldn't?"

Monsters

In Glasgow, Scotland, late at night, a taxi picked me up at a poet's house next to a park.

"Come along and sit inna front," the driver said. "If ye don't mind. Feels friendlier that way."

So I sat beside him, up on the left, which had started feeling normal after three weeks. He turned down the radio so we could talk.

"How ya doin?" he asked. "Where ya from?"

"Texas," I said. "And I'm sad. I'm sad to leave your country. I love your country and I'm leaving tomorrow. I don't want to leave, ever."

"Aye, but if ya love it, ye'll be back soon, no worries," said he. "It's a wee place, but some people like it. Glad ya do. I never saw Texas no way, never went ta the United States, but maybe someday. So who you visitin' in that neighborhood?"

"Poets," I said.

He seemed startled. "Aye, poets? I didn't know there were poets where I picked ye up."

"There are poets everywhere."

"Nah! Nah! Can't be true!"

We talked about the Open at Saint Andrew's and the Highlands and the Isle of Mull and Durness in the far northwest corner of the country where John Lennon the Beatle spent his summers as a little boy and those tasty pies called pasties and bridies and all sorts of Scottish wonders. I like Scottish highway signs: PLEASE ALLOW OVERTAKING—FRUSTRATION CAUSES ACCIDENTS and QUEUES LIKELY AHEAD and TIREDNESS CAN KILL.

I told him the poets said something very

interesting about politics. They said, "In Scotland, we never take ourselves too seriously, we're just a satellite of a monarchy, you know, so how could we? And we think that anyone who runs for a political office can't really have good intentions up his sleeve. Surely he or she is doing it for some ulterior motive. So we're pretty cynical in general about politics and if someone turns out to be good and honorable, we're pleasantly surprised. But you, in the United States, you *want* to believe in your politicians and that's why you're always so depressed and disappointed."

I thought that was great. I liked it even better, telling him.

"Aye," he said, eyeing me. "So are ye now? Depressed and disappointed?"

"About politics—totally."

"But you can vote fer somebody better next time, yes?"

"Yes, but see, we don't believe the votes are always

fair. And think of all the rotten things happening in the meantime. These things will take years to get over. I'm truly worried about the environment, aren't you? Yours here in Scotland looks better than most anywhere else. Say, do you believe in the Loch Ness monster?"

"Sure I do! Lotta other monsters, too. Highland monsters, deep cave monsters, sewer monsters, all kinda monsters."

I mentioned the nature god Pan who was supposed to prance around the gardens of giant cabbages up at Findhorn, near Inverness—half human, half goat. With little hooves and a small flute. I'd read about him a long time ago and wondered if he were still prancing. He wasn't a monster, though. He was more like a little fairy.

The taxi driver, who smelled like cabbages himself, and cigarettes, looked interested. "Might be!" he said. "I never hearda that wee one."

When I hopped out, he handed me his card for

next time and said, "Okay then, be safe to the other side of the sea."

I pressed the card up to my chest, and when he drove off I kissed it.

The person you have known a long time is embedded in you like a jewel.

The person you have just met casts out a few glistening beams and you are fascinated to see more of them. How many more are there?

With someone you've barely met the curiosity is intoxicating.

Brown

HOW MANY THINGS HAVE WE NEVER EVEN
thought about?

In a small Michigan village the young taxi driver who picked me up before dawn to drive me eighty miles to a town with an airport was driving a car that didn't look like a taxi at all. It looked like an old beat-up car a kid would drive. There was no meter or sign.

I said, "Are you really the taxi?"

He said, "No, I'm really a guy trying to make enough money to go to college and stay tanned, but they call me a taxi."

I threw my bags into the backseat with a bit of suspicion and climbed in, closing the dented door gingerly behind me. There were empty Gatorade bottles on the floor.

"Stay tanned?"

"Yeah. Tanning studio. I go three times a week. How often do you go?"

I laughed out loud. I couldn't help it. "Uh—I live in Texas. We could just go outside if we wanted to stay tanned. "

"Yeah, you're lucky. But I'm sure you have tanning studios down there, too. We have Tanzamillion."

"Yeah, sure we do—but . . . why? Why do you want to be tanned? It's not that healthy for you, is it?"

We were driving through fields of dark snow. A brilliant pink sun was just pushing up on the eastern horizon. I admired him for being up so early, anyway.

"It's important," he said. "For looks. You can't look good pale. I mean, you look healthier tan. You can also tan"—he turned his head to look at me—"places that never get tan otherwise."

Hmmmm. I didn't say, Thrilling. The butt and boob tans must be considered at all costs. It was a very odd conversation to be having before dawn.

I thought about my friend Trinidad Sanchez, Jr., who wrote a book of poems called *Why Am I So Brown?* I wished I had an extra copy with me to give to this dude. Wasn't it a little strange how racism in the world often worked against darker people, yet lighter people wanted to be darker? I knew that was not an original thought, but my driver caused it to surge back into my mind so early in the morning. He had spiky blond hair and the tattoo of a small cross on the side of his neck.

And he'd obviously had his caffeine. He kept talking, "It's pricey even when you buy a tan package. Like, I buy thirty tans at once, to get me through most of the winter, and that's a reduction, but still, it takes some bucks."

We were passing dark barns, silos, shadowy farm equipment pressed up against the sides of outbuildings. "Would you say that's one of your main expenditures?" (I was thinking books, food, movies, music, clothes, fuel. . . .)

"Yeah, pretty much so, I guess. It's not in the luxury category for sure. I put it in the basics. I don't know what people did before tanning studios. It is definitely a harder life for us up here in the north."

Rollentina

EVERYTHING IS ALWAYS BITS AND PIECES.

Everything is nickels and dimes and pennies and lost buttons and someone remembers the street called Durango from when he was a little boy and gets emotional just to see the sign.

Everything belongs to the one who passes, who sees it from the window—the yard sale sign and the crab shack sign and the church turned into a house and the raspberry stand in the back of a red truck. My friend Joe, driving along the coast of Deer Isle, Maine, says, "So there's nothing between us and

Scotland but some water and a few islands," and my whole heart shifts.

The driver at snowy Dorval Airport in Montreal says, "*Bonsoir,* Madame!" and opens the back door with a flourish.

I slide in, saying, "*Bonsoir* to you, too!" and feel like Archie Bunker.

The Korean taxi driver in Los Angeles says, "I will tell you where to find the best empanada, the best kimchee, the best eggplant rollentina, the best chipotle salsa fresh, the best shrimp pancake, the best . . ." He mixes cultures in a broad sweep of streets and there is nothing strange about it, nothing strange at all. "How do you know all this?" you ask him, and he sings, "I like to *eat*!"

Riding in a taxi, passing in a car, will always feel like the central human experience to me. Not graduating from high school or college, getting married, having a baby, no. Just passing in a car . . .

Once I picked up Tennessee Williams and

114

William Burroughs in the same car because my friend and I had offered to do some airport runs for a literary conference. The great writers said, "You're the taxi drivers, eh?" A heavy snow had fallen and my friend and I, who had no idea if Tennessee Williams and William Burroughs even got along or anything in real life, kept looking nervously at each other, hoping we wouldn't skid into a ditch. Neither one of us had expertise in driving in snow. The great writers were wearing heavy, dark overcoats and carrying briefcases. They chattered pleasantly in the backseat and didn't seem to notice that we drove very very slowly. To this day each one of us thinks we were the driver.

I can't forget riding in the back of a limousine in Philadelphia with the two most famous Palestinian intellectuals in the world, Edward Said and Mahmoud Darwish. I think we had bodyguards and bulletproof glass. Mariam Said, Edward's wife, was with us, and the great poet Carolyn Forché was there, too, and I knew even as this was happening that it was an incredible thing to be back there with them. Darwish had been sniffing our grand old hotel lobby as we all waited for the limo, saying, "This smells familiar! What does it smell like? It smells like—memory."

There was a part of my brain that could pole-vault out of that moment into a future moment and look back on it already and say, Oh my.

I felt tongue-tied. I could do nothing but listen and watch, observing two great men adjust their suit coats and converse and sip pure water from plastic bottles and make quiet jokes.

This is what I save—the elegant, unexpected moments that I slip into, like an envelope into a mailbox. I do not need there to be any message inside.

Test Case

BASICALLY CELL PHONES HAVE CHANGED everything in India. I am not sure whether this is good or bad. Probably it is a mixed curry.

I can't imagine that the dusty camel guides in the Thar Desert of far northwestern Rajasthan province have started using cell phones, because they didn't even have land lines twenty years ago, but the city of Delhi/New Delhi feels indelibly altered.

In the old days, like anywhere else, you had to guess if someone would show up where they promised, but now, you keep checking.

"Craft Museum? Hello? Ten minutes! Right-o!" or: "How is the traffic on your side of the city?" Terrible, of course. A city this giant, it's always terrible.

"Well, we're on our way! Save us a spot!"

The crowdedness is a beautiful terrible because it means life.

In Delhi everyone is very used to veering around strangely parked cars, broken buses, rickshaws, wandering cows, parades, flags, funeral processions, piles of junk, mounds of dirt and brick, small fires that people are heating large pots of water over, and heaps of giant pipes.

ROAD CLOSED is never a surprise.

A detour takes us through the heart of an impromptu shrine or under someone's personal clothesline flapping pink and orange scarves. We get into such a desperate traffic jam that a frustrated pedestrian tries to punch our driver through the open window. The driver yells back and rolls the window up. He shakes his head and says to us, "This man has no patience. It is not my fault that we are sitting here. Where can we go?"

We lock our doors.

A few hours later, after we have made fourteen detours and U-turns trying to locate a mysterious handmade paper store and I have purchased five packets of lime and orange envelopes, he turns his weary head and asks: "Do you mind if I take the new fly-over? I believe it will help us."

"What? Take it! Take anything!"

I picture the car spreading out wide wings and taking off. Fly-over? We would call it an overpass, looming up ahead of us, freshly white, sleek, and absolutely *empty*. Underneath us, on the old clogged roads, the traffic remains treacherously jammed, madly honking. We shoot up onto the smooth rise of concrete above them. Indeed, it is as if we are flying over everyone else.

"But why is no one else taking this road?" I ask

the driver as we look down on thousands of red blinking taillights.

He laughs nervously. "Because, Madam, this road is very new; it just opened last night. The workers have been building it for *years*. They had bad luck, and it took a long time, much longer than they thought it would take. So no one trusts it yet. They are thinking maybe it will be falling down. So they want to watch us to see what happens. We are the test case."

In the great and ancient city of Delhi, we are among the first to pass over a shining pavement. It doesn't fall. It's as if we came a few days ago, when the cement was wet, and pressed our fingers in.

Mouth of the Rat

"I AM NOT REALLY YOUR DRIVER. YOUR REAL driver is another person."

Why are people always telling me this?

When will we meet our real drivers?

"Your driver stopped to get gas and his car broke down. So he called me to pick you up instead. I am the driver of two other people arriving from New York. Can you wait till their plane lands? I brought a big car, it's parked outside, room enough for everybody. Come on, you can wait for us there."

We exit the baggage area together, entering the

sweet warm air of Florida. I breathe deeply and stare up at the stately palm trees for signs of hurricanes, but they look dignified, as if nothing bad has happened in their lives.

The driver-for-other-people leads me to an oversized white limousine.

"Wow," I say. I can tell he wants me to be impressed. He unlocks the door.

"There is plenty of room for all of us, see?"

I'd say. And those twelve people waiting for the shuttle, too.

"You can sit right here in the car while I wait for their plane. Check it out! Listen to the radio, watch TV. I'll be right back."

I never understand it when people think you wish to sit again after you have been sitting for hours. It's like being in school. Sit forever. But I don't want to insult him, since we've just met. And he isn't really my driver. So I climb in. He turns the key of the giant car and leaves the limo running so I don't suffocate inside. He goes back into the airport.

I would rather open the windows, but they don't seem to be working. I spin the dials on everything. The TV doesn't work. The radio is static on every station. No drinks in the little limo-coolers. That is always a hope in a limousine. Icy drinks stashed in the built-in box. But this is a run-down limo, that's for sure. All for show. I'm not fond of these gas guzzlers anyway. Who needs them? People going to proms. Politicians conducting high-dollar secret business deals. Sports stars. But me, in my rumpled flying clothes? Get me out of here.

Then I remember. Isn't Florida the state with so many carjackings?

Not to be suspicious or anything, but might a running limousine with one tired person in the back be alluring to someone with carjacking on the brain?

I get out very quickly, climb into the front seat, turn off the key. Lock the limo, put the key in my pocket. For pretty darn sure it is the only time in my life I will have a limo key in my pocket.

I stare up at the twilight sky of West Palm Beach and sniff the soft air which smells like pineapple and Hawai'i and coconut milk and say, "Hello Florida. Helloooooo West Palm Beach." My destination is Boca Raton, Mouth of the Rat. I meditate for a while on the weird names of places and invent some. Stew Pot, West Virginia. Shoelace, Texas. Messed Up but Still Beloved, Louisiana.

I get a call on my cell phone. My friend John in Knoxville says, "Hey. Hey, I just saw a church marquee you won't believe. Here it is: WHAT IF JESUS SAID, I DON'T LOVE YOU ANYMORE, YOU DON'T MAKE ME HAPPY, I'VE FOUND SOMEONE ELSE."

About forty-five minutes later the driver returns, dragging the giant suitcases of an older, travel-weary couple wearing expensive gray coats.

I have started directing traffic by now. I have guided a black limousine carrying NBA stars into a space right next to me. I have bowed and waved to women picking up their husbands. I have made peace signs to little kids.

The driver stares at me. Why am I standing outside of the car? I say, "I didn't want to waste all your gas." He smiles and I hand him back his key.

I don't say, *Idling makes me feel like vomiting. I didn't want to get carjacked.*

The couple stares at me with mild displeasure. They seem to dislike the idea of sharing their car, especially with someone so disheveled. I shrug and say, "Sorry I have to ride with you all. He is not my real driver. My driver is lost in action."

The wife looks to her husband for a response. He sighs and says nothing. Am I not the one who should be irritated? Thanks to my lost driver and this couple's late plane, I have forfeited relaxation time in my beachside hotel. I sit as far away from them as I can in the huge interior. How will we turn this into fun?

As we speed along, I begin interrogating them.

It's just too awkward to sit in gloomy silence. "How was your flight? What was the weather like in New York? Pretty big coats you have there!" They answer in muffled monosyllables for about ten miles. I gather they live half the time in Florida and half the time in New York. Grumble, grumble. The problems of so many keys . . . Their grandchildren live in Florida. They attend many parties and kiddie social activities down here. She's wearing pearls and posh earrings. They're glad to be back. Sigh. New York was feeling very tiresome recently. The man walks three miles daily when he's in Florida. In New York he's a surgeon with a high-pressure schedule, but down here he's a walker with a jaunty cap. I ask them about "mouth of the rat." Why such a name for any town? Something to do with the shape of a bay, they say. They put their heads together very closely when they talk. I imagine they are grumbling privately about my inquiries.

We pass lavish pink-frilled mansions with dramatic stucco arches, ornate wrought-iron balconies, and circular driveways. The woman says, "No one really lives there. Those houses are tax write-offs. Too big for their own good."

Sort of like this car.

The driver never says a word. He's up there in his own country, at the wheel.

"So where are you staying?" the woman asks me reluctantly (*we don't really want to know more about this person but she won't shut up*) and I name a hotel. They know it. They say, "It's a very nice hotel," but it won't be, at all. It will be truly mediocre—stinky elevators, saggy mattresses, a restaurant smelling of Clorox, and the same bad news of the world on the television screen.

The couple chitchat comfortably about the dinner they will have once they unpack. Will they go out? Will they eat something frozen from their freezer? They mention phone calls they forgot to make before leaving. "Oh dear," she frets, "that just slipped out of my mind!"

"We'll call them from here," says the surgeon.

I want to tell them to go out. Have fun. Wind down. Ever since I was a kid I have had to restrain myself from giving unsolicited advice. I think it says something bad about character that this is such a temptation. Who do I think I am? Telling other people how to live their lives. No wonder some of my own relatives won't speak to me anymore.

We pass a Bad to the Bone Barbeque restaurant. "Now that's a good place!" the surgeon says.

I say, "Especially if you're a surgeon," and he actually laughs.

I say, "Do you keep a car down here?" and they say, "Oh, of course we do. How else would we get anywhere? It's not like New York, where you just hail a taxi and go anywhere you want."

They are loosening up. I can feel their muscles

lengthening. She says, "I am so impressed at the ways palm trees can bend," and he says, "They don't show the strain of the storms at all." I say, "That's just what I was thinking about as I waited for you!" They take deep breaths, and he pats her hand.

When we reach their tall, glittering, silver condominium building, they gather their gloves and newspapers excitedly and climb out into their Florida lives. Their full southern pep has returned. The driver helps them haul their baggage inside and they call back to me, "Have a great time, sweetie!"

The sun has set—I like the succulent blackness of Florida night seeping in through the open door. It feels like a tonic. When the driver closes the door and gets back in, I say to him, "They were nice."

He turns his head sharply and snaps, "Ha! Once you got them going. Don't believe for a minute they're normal, though. They were faking it. They tried to act normal, but really they're spoiled millionaires. I know their kind; I see them all the time. They are not normal at all."

Sightseeing

AT SEVEN A.M. IN SAN ANTONIO, A SHORT-haired white cat sits straight up on the hood of a dusty green car in the parking lot of the Sanitary Tortilla Factory.

A man stands near the car staring at the cat, smiling.

In my bicycle basket a brown paper bag of thin corn tortillas lies steaming hot. It costs sixty cents. There's nothing better than fresh corn tortillas with scrambled eggs and a few fried onions and peppers.

I can't resist circling in the parking lot to look

more closely at the cat. He has an incredibly observant gaze. He is staring at sparrows hopping around on the pavement.

"Good morning," I call out to the man. "Say, what are you two doing?"

Pointing at the cat, the man says, "He likes to ride around. Get a different view. He's just looking."

The cat seems to be sniffing, too.

"Is he your cat?"

"My wife's cat. We ride around every day. I park, and he gets out and takes a look. He likes it."

There's a green Dumpster with a wide mouth. A red hand-lettered HELP WANTED sign on the door of the factory. An old stone church ringing its bell across the street. This is the oldest tortilla factory still operating in the city.

"How many places do you go every day?"

"Oh, four or five each morning. I vary the routine. He likes some places more than others."

"How did you figure out that he wanted to do this?"

"He always sat on the front porch step and stared very sadly at me and the car when I drove off without him. So one day I let him come with me and we started our tradition."

The man makes a little click with his tongue, and the cat gracefully steps over the car mirror and hops through the open window back onto the passenger seat.

The man smiles at me and shrugs. "Now we'll go somewhere else."

Tips

WELL, I WALKED DOWN TO THE PIKE PLACE Market in Seattle and the yellow flowers were still fat, the fishmongers were still pitching and slapping the fish. I stayed in a cool hotel called Hotel Max that had giant black-and-white Seattle photographs on all the doors of the rooms. Every photograph was different. My room had a dog, peering around a corner. There was a note on the table by my bed that said I could order cold buckwheat noodles in a bowl any hour of the day or night, and they were pretty cheap, too.

My visit to the international teachers' conference went well, but the taxi back to the airport, which we had booked three hours in advance, didn't show up. Someone called it again for me as I stood by the curb and waited for forty minutes. I was waiting by a blue bench and a crossing light, just where they told me to wait. I was starting to get worried. No other empty taxis passed, so I couldn't hail one. Salmon trucks passed, and dairy trucks, and buses filled with interesting-looking people I would never meet, and young moms with babies in car seats. Then I overheard a woman who had just shown up half a block down the curb saying, "Airport" to a taxi driver as he swooped up to her, so I hustled over there and said, "Maybe you're here for Nye?" and he said, "No, I'm here for Martin." I asked if I could join them and pay half. They nodded. "Now I'll get a really good tip," the driver said.

Very quickly I could bet the Martin woman was glad I rode with her because the driver rambled

nonstop from downtown to the airport and it's eas-
ier to have two people in the backseat saying "Uh-
huh" and "Mmmmm" instead of just one. We
could take turns.

He started by pointing at the jail and then just
went on from there, like someone had flipped a
switch.

*You ladies don't want to check into that hotel I'll bet,
heh heh heh! Not even a good spot to have lunch, I'd
say, though Seattle has a million kinda restaurants if
you're hungry and every cuisine you could dream of
even weird stuff from weird countries you didn't know
existed like Zanzibania and I was wondering, have you
ladies ever tasted one of our great northwestern special-
ties, the Rainier cherry, the one that is yellow more than
red and very tart and delicious?* (Uh-huh.)

*You have? Oh well I was going to go to a fruit stand
on the way to the airport and get you a bunch of them
in a paper sack if you'd never tasted them, do you by
any chance remember what you paid per pound?*

(Mmmmm, maybe $3.99? Or $4.99? Pretty expensive . . .)

Oh wow they're much cheaper here of course near the source of the trees I guess that's how it always goes, things cheaper near their sources, or is it? (Mmmmm) *I heard something about how the clothes made in China aren't cheap in China if you could even buy them there but they're for export only so usually you can't.* (He points at a building.) *Do you ladies realize that that building of forty stories was, for many years, the tallest building west of the Mississippi?* (We did not.) *Do you know who owned it?* (Huh-uh.) *Mr. Smith. And can you guess which Mr. Smith he was?* (Mmmmm. No telling.) *Can you ladies guess which product it was that made him rich? I'll bet you can, you got some years on you heh heh heh. It's an office tool. That's my only hint.* (He taps his wedding ring on the steering wheel.) *Think of it ladies, it's a sound that teenagers of today will never know, I feel a little sorry for them. . . .* (Smith Corona! I shout.) *You got it!*

Right-o! (He honks madly. Two cars swerve out of his lane.) *I think you should get a prize for that, okay I'll tell you something else, we have a Concorde and we have Lyndon Johnson's airplane and we have a DC-3 hanging from the ceiling and guess where they are? Have you ever been there? Our Museum of Flight! It's a must for your next trip. Lots of people miss it. They always go to the dad-gum Pike Place Market and the first Starbucks like big deal who cares about a coffee shop even if it did start here.* (Mmmmm you could say that again.) *I could take you a place where a cuppa coffee's still fifty cents and it's a good one too in a big mug. Anyway back to the flight museum, I guess if you fly a lot yourselves you might not be that excited to go to a Museum of Flight right off but trust me those of us that stay on the ground really get into it. The pilot of the Concorde did not make any friends in this town when he delivered the plane though, he was supposed to land around three-thirty but he arrived early at two-fifteen because he took a shortcut over Canada from wherever he was coming from and all the little kids that had permission to get out of school to see it land and were on their way over here in big yellow schoolbuses missed it. When they got here it was just sitting on the runway like no big deal and the engine was already turned off. And the kids didn't even want to deliver those welcome cards they had made, the newspaper wrote about them, welcome cards to an airplane, they could hardly stick them on the nose of the plane. . . .*

Lending Library

I'M FASCINATED BY THE TRAIN OF THOUGHT.
How many cars does it have?

In San Jose, California, a driver waited for my
late plane for three hours. I wished no one had been
called in advance and I could just have found someone on the spot. He hauled my suitcase grumpily,
trying to be professionally gracious, but it was clear
he was bummed out in the pouring rain. I apolo-
gized profusely. "I thought you would have left me
by now." He had driven in something like seventy
miles from Monterey. I explained that all million

passengers at DFW airport had been evacuated from the entire place, every terminal and gate, after some nutty college student ran through a security checkpoint without stopping. It took quite a while to get us all checked back in.

The driver didn't want to hear about it. He wanted to know what I was reading. He had a book in his own pocket. "Reading saved me tonight," he said.

"Reading always saves me," I said.

"Right on!" he said. Things seemed to be improving.

It was raining so hard I asked if it was a monsoon and he said no. He said, "I'll read a *TV Guide* if I have nothing else. And I don't watch TV."

"I wouldn't go *that* far."

I told him I was reading Peter Matthiessen's *Lost Man's River* on the plane, while I was feeling somewhat lost, and he got very happy.

"Matthiessen is the best!!!" he said. "*Far Tortuga* is my favorite novel of all time! And *The Snow*

Leopard is my best nonfiction book—so what are the odds of the same person writing your favorite book in both genres?"

"Pretty cool."

And then, because he was so excited, I couldn't help myself.

"Have you met him?" I asked.

"Are you kidding? I wish!"

"Well, I have. In fact, I know him. I know his wonderful wife and I have stayed at their home."

"Are you joking?" Now he was happy he'd waited for me.

Sometimes name-dropping comes in handy in this world. The trick is knowing when.

"Where is his house?"

I told him in general terms. I told him Peter's wife had a huge, gorgeous garden and a cozy kitchen filled with beautiful pans and kettles, and they had a fireplace and a million books.

He asked me when I had first read *The Snow*

Leopard. "In college," I said. "It marked me."

He said, "YO! My whole life shifted into a different gear when I read that book."

"What do you mean?"

"I got more honest," he said. "I wanted to live my life in a more meaningful way. So this is what I decided to do and it became my regular pattern—work for a year and explore for a year. I wouldn't get married or have kids and I wouldn't build up any material empire or anything—I would just save my money by living very simply for a whole year, then spend it on the road for the next year. So here are the places I have seen—Morocco, Egypt, Indonesia, Thailand, Siberia, China, Bhutan, Turkey, Lebanon, Argentina, Chile, Samoa, New Zealand. Next year I'll be hiking in France for the whole year. I really haven't spent much time in Europe yet. It's more expensive. But I can truly say *The Snow Leopard* sent me to all these places. Would you tell Peter that for me?"

"You bet," I said. "He'll like it."

"Oh—and I'm hoping for Antarctica, too. But I have to find an affordable way to do that."

"I like your life."

He said, "I'm never lonely. And I've only taken a friend along twice. But I always take books and find more books. . . . Say, have you read another one of my truly favorite books, *Cold Oceans* by Jon Turk?"

"No."

"Well, give me your address and I'll send it to you. I have three copies that I loan out. But you have to send it back to me in three months. Promise?"

"Maybe I can find it on my own so you don't have to bother."

"No! I'd rather send it. It will change your life. It's about Jon Turk's adventures in a kayak, a rowboat, and on a dogsled."

"I'll stick with the rowboat," I say. "We rode on a

dogsled once in the Alaskan tundra and I thought I was going to launch to outer space. Very bumpy and a little too thrilling for me. Also, my son kept thinking the dogs were going to bite us."

"Well, read this book and live vicariously. Write your address down right now! You'll see the book in your box when you get back home. So when are you going home?"

I gave him a triple big tip, for waiting so long, and "for France." He sent Turk's book. I loved it. It didn't make me want to take a kayak or anything, but I couldn't put it down. I sent it back swiftly with a thank you letter and my own list of favorite exploration books by different authors. And I sent a vintage bon voyage card that I found in my mysterious stationery drawer—to the man who learned early how he wanted to live, then did it.

No Room at the Inn

IT'S A TERRIBLE FEELING WHEN THE DESK clerk at a hotel says they gave your room away to somebody else. Especially when you just got off a plane, it's dark, and you're tired.

"But I have a confirmation number," you say.

The clerk says, "Sorry. We gave it away."

Then the kicker. "Hate to tell you this, but there is no hotel room available in the entire city of Chicago. That's why we gave all the reserved rooms away in the last few hours. Due to the huge restaurant convention which is being attended by all the restaurant people of Canada and Europe as well as the United States, every single room in the city is taken. We have made a reservation for you in another town and will pay a taxi driver to take you there right now."

Another town? I can't go to another town. I have to work here, very close to this hotel, beginning at nine A.M. tomorrow, which now seems very soon.

I'm distracted by another thought. Are all the restaurants of the world closed right now? If the managers are gathered in Chicago, who is running the restaurants?

The desk clerk motions discreetly to the concierge, who grabs my bags and runs off with them to a waiting taxi. This feels like a conspiracy. The clerk thrusts three tens and a five into my hand and says, "Pay the taxi with this. We'll tell him where to take you."

I'm stunned. Then I'm in the taxi's backseat and he's pulling out into the street.

"Okay then," says the driver with an Indian accent. "We will be going."

I stutter, "Where is this place you are taking me? I have to work tomorrow very early at the Chicago Art Institute. I do not wish to leave the city. How far away is this other place, actually?"

He says, "Madame, I cannot tell you that. You are the first person I have ever taken there. A while ago I took some other guests to Evanston, but I am not sure of this place I am taking you. The hotel wrote down directions for me."

"Did those other people *want* to go to Evanston?"

"They did not."

"Don't you think this is a little strange? How far away do you think the place is?"

"I don't know. Twenty miles, maybe."

"Terrible! Do you really think there are no hotel rooms available in all of Chicago?"

"That is what I hear. Other drivers were talking about this over the radio; it seems to be accurate."

"I can't believe it."

"It is difficult to believe. But what can we do?"

We drive and drive, beyond the glittering neon late-night cafés and under the tall legs of the elevated railway where I would prefer to unfold my tent, if I had one. Should I ask him to stop at the hotels we are passing? Suddenly I feel exhausted. Surely that nasty hotel would have sent me to a closer place if they could. I take some deep breaths to calm down. I give myself a frenzied hand massage, one thumb pressing the base of the other thumb. Everywhere hurts. Certainly I have friends in Chicago, but I can hardly call them at this late hour and don't have their numbers with me anyway. Nor do I have a cell phone yet.

So I say, "Are you from India?"

The driver says, "Yes! How did you guess?"

We talk about India. When I am feeling gloomy about one thing, I try to ask questions about another thing. If a plane flight becomes excessively turbulent, for example, I grow extremely curious about my seatmate's job history, even if he is a banker or a purveyor of medical tools.

This driver and I, forging into the ominous darkness together, discuss the south and north of India, the vivid, spicy curries, the quirky Bird Hospital in old downtown Delhi, the Red Fort, an Indian circus we once saw where a small, weeping bear was forced to dance with a teacup on his head, and the sand dunes of the Thar Desert, where my husband and I once rode camels for days, feeling suspended in the vastness of space. My husband and I stopped calling out to each other after the first few hours, soaking and baking in silence, and we slept in a tiny village, in a manger filled with rank hay and the warm breath of sheep. We may have used small lambs as pillows or I may have made that up. Anyway, we survived it. Although my husband grew very ill afterward, we did not die.

The taxi is now out of the city, on a dark two-lane

road, passing between groves of tall trees. When did we exit the interstate?

"Tell me about your family," I say, trying to quell my uneasiness about the distance and the dark.

"I am worried about my daughter," he jumps right in. "She is caught between two cultures, the old and the modern. She is trying to find her way. It is hard to keep traditional Hindu culture alive when you are surrounded by so many influences and distractions. We moved to the United States from India when she was nine—now she is sixteen, and often seems confused."

I say, "Everyone is confused when they are sixteen."

He says, "She wants things."

I say, "Everyone wants things when they are sixteen. But don't we all want things? I want to be in Chicago, for example, not on this back road to—where are we now exactly?"

He says, "Frankly, I do not know."

There are no signs, no markers, no lights—a

suddenly desolate region. Maybe we have entered a national park wilderness. Lake Michigan Nowhere. If he did not seem to be such an honorable Hindu, I might feel more edgy. He appears to be gripping the wheel very tightly now. He says, "It is truly dark here. She watches television constantly."

Squinting to read my watch in the dark, I see it is ten-fifty P.M. I cannot imagine how I am going to make it back to the Art Institute by nine A.M., and I am furious.

Take a deep breath. I say, "Television is very violent. Does she watch nice shows?"

He says, "How can I know what she watches? I am away from home all the time, driving a taxi to make a living. I fear the music channel and the naked shows. My wife is working in a school as an aide, then a second job in a Dollar Shop for extra dollars. She begs our children not to watch television, but they feel distance from their friends if they do not do what their friends are doing."

I feel distance from everyone I have ever known on earth.

I say, "Is your wife at home right now?"

He says, "I would certainly hope so."

Trees and more trees, ferocious, shadowy tree-silence looming in all directions, and not a signal or scrap of sign to go by.

I say, "Sir, it seems to me we have been driving thirty minutes by now. Would you say so?"

"Yes."

I say, "Could we please take the first turnoff to anywhere? It will be impossible for me to get back into the city early enough in the morning. I am having a nervous breakdown, and I suggest we exit immediately."

He says, "Madam, I am sorry for your condition."

"I am Naomi, by the way."

"Madam Naomi, I am Rajiv. As in Ghandi, but not quite."

We do not see an exit or another street to turn

onto for at least ten more miles. He says, "It seems we have found the last forgotten place."

I say, "It is imperative that we get advice. The hotel idiot gave me thirty-five dollars to pay you and already your meter says sixty-five dollars. Of course you must be paid fully, considering the fact that you have a long way to drive home as well. I am feeling quite grim."

Rajiv says, "I will stop wherever you tell me."

Finally a restaurant looms out of the dark, rimmed with festive red lights around the edge of the roof and a blinking sign: LORENZO'S ITALY.

"Here! Stop."

Rajiv turns off the taxi and comes into the restaurant with me, after locking the doors.

A woman swabbing down the counter inside the restaurant lobby says, "I'm sorry, we're closed."

"I'm sure you are," I say. "As well you should be. We just need help please. We are lost and we are very upset."

She rings a bell and a large man steps out of the kitchen. He looks at us curiously. "I am the manager. May I help you?"

"Lorenzo?"

"No, Jack. Lorenzo's the owner. He's not here."

He's probably at the restaurant convention.

Rajiv shows Jack the ragged scrap of paper on which our directions are scrawled. Jack reads the address and looks pensive. "But why are you here if you want to go there? You're lost! This hotel they wrote down is on a different road from this one and it's not very close to here, either. Hate to tell you that. Hmmmm. You can get there, though. It will take a while."

We tell him the whole horrible story in a few choked sentences. I say, "I could just start crying." Rajiv looks deeply worried. He excuses himself and steps into the restroom.

Jack says, "Wait a minute, please. " He disappears back into the kitchen. He probably doesn't want to be alone with me.

When Jack returns, he is carrying five fragrant brown paper bags with handles, shopping bag size. He says, "I can't house you, but I can feed you. Here is pasta Alfredo, our specialty, and two spinach and mushroom pizzas and eggplant Parmesan with a little garlic and herb pasta on the side and spaghetti and meatballs and bread sticks and salads. I think they put some lasagna in there, too. I hope you will enjoy it."

I say, "You are incredibly nice. This is unbelievable." I hug him. He smells like comforting garlic, like my dad when he helps in the kitchen. Rajiv looks confused. Jack gives Rajiv more directions. Rajiv scribbles them wildly on the same paper, on the back. I think he writes them in Sanskrit. We climb into the car with our vast trove of Italian cuisine and drive off into the night.

"But are you hungry?" I ask Rajiv.

"No, thank you."

"I will insist that you take this food home with

you for your daughter and wife and family."

"No, certainly not. It was given to you."

"It should feed you for about a week or more," I say.

Rajiv says, "Jack was very nice. I am not partial to Italian food, however. I will only take half of it. My daughter likes spaghetti."

"I will write Jack a thank you letter from both of us. I picked up a business card off the counter."

After quite a few more miles, after turning where Jack told us to turn—profoundly subtle turns which we would never have discovered on our own—we find our despicable destination. "Stay here a moment," I beg Rajiv. "Please, you must wait. What if you leave me and they don't have room for me either?"

"I will be waiting." He sighs.

I speak to the desk clerk as I would speak to a life-guard if I had just been hauled out of the deep end of a pool. "I need you to help me," I gasp. "Tell me you have a room reserved in my name and how long do you think it will take to get back into Chicago during rush hour in the morning?"

She chews her gum. "A long time. Yeah, we have your name. You came from the Fairmont, yeah."

"Not by choice, trust me."

"They called."

"I hate them."

When I go back to the sidewalk to collect my baggage, Rajiv has lined all five food bags next to my two pieces of luggage and is standing there looking very sad.

"Please," he says. "Just take it all."

"What am I going to do with it? You have a family! I can't carry seven bags!"

I plop three of the bags on his backseat.

"Here, you promised. We split the bounty."

I pay him one hundred dollars, planning to force the Fairmont to pay me back the difference. He says, "The Fairmont only gave you thirty-five dollars, I can't take this much."

"Oh please," I say. "We've been driving for hours. Consider it a tip. In fact, if you don't take it and beat it out of here, I'm going to make you drive me back into Chicago in the morning."

"I am going now. I actually live on the south side of Chicago. It will take me twice as long to get there as it took us to get here. If I can find it."

"I am so sorry."

"And I am also sorry. It was not your fault. It was no one's fault."

"You're wrong; it was someone's fault. And I am going to go call them right now. Thank you for being so nice to me and not tying me to a tree. Good luck to your daughter. Drive carefully."

"I will eat a salad," says Rajiv.

"Viva Italia!" I say. But no one laughs. It is impossible to be funny at this time of night.

And I realize, after unlocking my shoddy Clorox-scented room and unpacking one of the food bags, that I have all the salads. Rajiv must have the pizzas. I actually sit and eat a salad. I close my eyes, tasting the vinegar, the lovely olives, the Parmesan-crusted croutons.

Then I dial the Fairmont.

"Manager, please."

When the manager comes on, I summarize the story, ending with:

"You will pay for this. You owe me for the taxi. You will also pay for the taxi I have to take to get back into Chicago. Do you understand the word *confirmation*? I am occasionally a travel writer and will not hesitate to call your hotel by its full name in whatever I write. I will not mince words. This is not a picnic."

Actually, it has turned into something of a picnic, food sprawled all over the bedspread, but I do not tell him that part.

The manager stutters. He says he was not on duty when all this happened. He says he will personally send a taxi to pick me up at seven A.M.

The next morning, after a grim night under the garlicky polyester bedspread, I eat a bread stick for breakfast. A taxi is miraculously waiting. A driver from Bosnia, with a square blond head, drives me back into the city. He says, "This is strange place to be staying. How you find it?"

I growl. I am sure he knows stories that are much worse. I ask if he could possibly be interested in fettucini at this early hour and he says no.

At the Fairmont, as the desk clerk is counting out tens to pay me back, I learn the penthouse has been reserved for me. *The penthouse*. Gratis. I may check in after three P.M.

"We are terribly sorry about your inconvenience."

I go to work at the Chicago Art Institute, where the newsletter has mistakenly broadcast that my preferred poetry workshop audience age is two.

Luckily one of the curators has a guitar in a back closet. I sit on the carpeted floor against the wall, singing kooky songs, while three two-year-olds comb my hair and one plays with my shoes. There are about fifty of them in the room. I have never been with so many two-year-olds at once in my life.

Back at the penthouse, I iron my shirt for the evening's reading, hoping the audience is old enough to read. I stare out the window at beautiful, glittering Chicago, first favorite city of my life. I wrote my Poem Number One here, at six, in a hotel. Not this hotel. Another one. It's dust.

I wander around and stare at my glamorous quarters. The hotel is doing penance now. They are afraid of vengeful travel writers, apparently. I enjoy the complimentary plate of crackers and cheese, the purple grapes. I pack the wine to take home to my husband. And I stare out the window, wishing Rajiv and Jack and Rajiv's daughter could join me for a little toast to fortune, the down and up of it, in this room with so many channels, above the deep and silent lake.

Bruce

THE YOUNGISH DRIVER WITH CURLY BLOND hair at Newark Airport says he has lived most of his life in New Jersey, so I ask if he likes Bruce Springsteen. It's a little dumb, I guess. Is he going to ask if I like Willie Nelson next?

But he's so happy I asked! "Bruce is my main man! I've even been out to his farm to pick up some of his band members! He was doing yard work off in the distance like a regular guy, isn't that crazy? I almost passed out at the wheel when I saw him. I even know the license plate number of his black

Land Rover by heart! I can't believe you asked me that!"

I say, "Well, I always think of him in New Jersey. I've been a big fan of Bruce since 1973."

"No way! Same here! Me, too! The E Street Band!"

"You don't look that old," I say.

"Neither do you! Neither does he, come to think about it. Neither does *anybody*."

I say, "Bruce is the fountain of youth."

We talk about Bruce's recordings of Pete Seeger songs and his concerts during the Kerry campaign. I say, "I just clipped a Bruce quotation out of the newspaper and stuck it to my wall with tape. 'When it comes to luck, you make your own.'"

"That sounds like Bruce," he says.

I say, "I know some guys that fly all around the country just to hear him perform live. I think I've heard him three times. I never saw anyone on stage with more energy, did you?"

"Never! He's the best!" We rave back and forth over the shiny seat. We're juiced on Bruce. I tell him our son memorized the entire *Tunnel of Love* album when he was two and used to sing it loudly, even in inappropriate moments. He says, "No way! Well, my wife and I played only Bruce songs at our wedding reception a few years ago. It was outdoors. We blasted them. She didn't really know that much about him when we first met, but I converted her."

I say, "So did you get out of the car that day at his farm and fall on your knees in front of him?"

He laughs and sighs. "Unfortunately not. Wish I had, though. I meet celebrities all the time, so I'm very subtle. I can't show my feelings. I'm a fly on the wall."

"Do you drive them around?"

"Yes! I work for another agency that specializes in celebrity service. I only do this taxi thing half-time. Want me to tell you some insider stuff? Just don't use my name if you tell anyone else."

"You bet. Tell me! Do I even know your name? How could I use it?"

"Oh, right. Okay, Kevin Bacon is very nice and low-key. He's a sweetheart. Down-home guy. I could ride around with him all day. Seinfeld used to be nice, but he changed. Bad sign when people start acting spoiled. James Taylor is a super good guy. Just like you'd think. Some musicians are really touchy, though. Especially jazz musicians, surprisingly. I would have thought they'd be nicer. I mean, jazz is loose. But they're not loose. Sometimes musicians hum in the backseat. I like that. Gives me a groove."

He roars through a yellow light and continues telling. "Julia Roberts is guarded. Doesn't want to say much. Always sinking into her collar like you might take notes on her or something. John Travolta is fabulous. Talk, talk, talk! He loves flying more than anything. You can drive him around and completely forget he's a star. But then there are people—ohmygod—the last time I was asked to pick up Donald Trump, I refused. Gave the job to someone else. My blood pressure won't take it."

He pauses.

I say, "Arrogance is a drag."

He says, "Big drag." Then he says, "One more thing. If you like Tom Cruise, get out of this car."

"I don't care for Tom Cruise."

"Good! Then you can stay in. He follows a religion invented by a science fiction writer, for pete's sake! And acts pompous about it! But worse than that, he thinks he's so *cute*. I can't stand it when a man his age thinks he's cute. A twenty-year-old staring at himself in a window is okay, but a man his age? All those leather jackets and shit. Excuse me. He really burns me up."

A million non-celebrities are outside walking on the sidewalks, carrying packages of hot dog buns, reams of paper, coffee cups, walking jumpy little dogs, catching glimpses of themselves in windows.

Some of them probably think they are very cute. And they are.

He says, "Sometimes talking or thinking about stars puts me in a bad mood. Why can't they just be happy and nice to people? They have everything. Looks, talent, money, glory. Still, they beat up on people, cheat on their wives, throw telephones . . . ho-hum. Bruce is a *true* star. Let's only talk about Bruce. If I ever get to drive him somewhere, I am seriously going to have to find a way to tell him what he means to me. I just hope I won't be tongue-tied." He pauses. "The other thing that gets me in a bad mood is talking about our government. Don't even get me started."

"I won't. It's beyond speaking."

"It's too much."

"We love Bruce."

Fun with Grandpa

I DIAL MY FATHER UP IN NORTH TEXAS TO speak to my only child, who's visiting his grandparents for the weekend. My dad says, "Hey, we're driving down a country road right now on the way to buy ice cream. We can't really talk."

I say, "Can I speak with him?"

My dad says, "Well, he's in the back of the truck. I can't reach him from here."

"DAD!" I say. "Isn't it against the law to ride in the back of a pickup truck?"

He says, "Maybe, but we're going slow. He likes it."

"Yeah, but you're driving with one hand, too."

My dad pulls over on some country road between cattle in fields, gets out of the driver's seat, and hands the phone to my son in the back. I can hear the truck start up again and a lot of fumbling going on with the phone.

"Hey!" I say to my son. "Would you please get in the cab? Pound on the back window and make him stop again and get in the cab."

He doesn't reply to this at all but says, "Say, Mom, we ran over a snake with the riding lawn mower this morning. It was really big and the grass was tall so we didn't see it. It was huge, actually, it was *gigantic*. Must have been a rattlesnake for sure. Then we had to get it off the blades. Poor guy, it was all mangled, wasn't quite dead yet either. Oof! Sorry, Grandpa hit a bump. Everything is fine! We're having a great time!"

Free Day in Toronto

A JOURNALIST WHO ATE A ROTTEN FIG FOUR days ago is in the emergency room.

A suave Portuguese man (easy to picture him on a cell phone in an airport, conducting distant business deals) feels his esophagus flaming. He says he has recently lost twenty pounds, and vomits without warning. Instead of flying up for the weekend to his cottage on Lake Superior where the water is so clean you can swim and drink at the same time, he came to the emergency room.

I diagnose him right away. "Some amoeba, from

drinking the lake!" He shakes his head. They already tested him for it.

An older woman who fell and hit her head on a concrete step is here, wearing gigantic dark glasses. Her worried husband hovers over her.

Three daughters are translating for their mother speaking some melodious Asian language (I feel ashamed not to know which one). The mother's high fever keeps recurring. The daughters say she won't leave the house. They had to drag her here.

"Why *won't* she leave the house?" asks Dr. Ovens, who attends to us one by one in a gentle, round-robin fashion, as we wait on high stretcher beds fanning out from Emergency's central computer.

The daughters speak to their mother. They shake their heads.

"She just won't leave the house. She has no energy."

Think of it. Toronto, a glossy, high-chrome and glass city, surging with subways and taxis, versus a listless, overheated immigrant who doesn't speak English. Why would she feel like going out?

An attractive young woman wearing a strappy flowered sundress is crying. Her tall boyfriend leans over her bed and whispers in her ear. She doesn't look sick. She looks *disturbed.*

Everyone keeps asking everyone else if it is *still raining.* What are they talking about? It has not rained a drop all week! How long have they been in here?

Old magazines I missed are lying around on bedside tables. Touching tattered magazines in an emergency unit feels slightly dangerous. But I am so happy to find Dave Eggers's 1999 account of picking up hitchhikers in Cuba, I'm almost glad to have come here. Dave drove around the island of Cuba in a rented VW van. He picked up anyone with a thumb out. People took him home, served him rice and beans and rum, and he learned about Cuba from the inside out. I want to go to Cuba and rent a car and become a free-for-all taxi driver as soon as I can. But I will have to fly from Canada, not from the U.S., or I will get *arrested*.

Another duo has joined us in the den of emergencies—a fragile, sad-faced mother, perhaps eighty-five, with bouffant blond hair and a pretty white blouse, supporting herself on a walker, and her son, about sixty, dressed as if for golf, fanning a sheaf of papers and yelling at her, *yelling, yelling,* because she made some questionable investments and the *numbers do not go together*!

"Mercy me," says the head-hitter's husband. "Could you please take this up at the bank? We are suffering here!"

"Cool it!" hisses the boyfriend. "You are upsetting my girlfriend!"

"Sir," says the nurse, "if you don't lower your voice, we'll have to ask you to leave."

"I think," the husband whispers to me, "he's worried she's going to pop her top and his inheritance won't be in order."

* * *

"Why are you here?" Jennifer the nurse asks me. She is placing little EKG buds all over my chest and shoulders. She has sleek rectangular glasses, a gray T-shirt, and a warm, genuine presence. I would like to have lunch with her or sit beside her on a plane. I would like to drive her around Cuba.

She doesn't just mean my medical condition, she means *in Toronto.*

My son and I have been attending a children's literature conference at a university campus for a week. Today was to be our one free sightseeing day.

We had discussed renting bicycles to ride along the harbor front. We had not yet sampled the bubble tea (tapioca grains floating in frothy brew) or seen Greektown or visited the shoe museum.

"Children's literature!" says Jennifer. "I adore children's literature! My daughter's seventeen. I love William Steig!"

I say, "Coincidentally, we were just talking about

his book *Dr. DeSoto* in the cab on the way over here."

"In the cab? Why?"

"It must have been prophetic."

The minute my EKG is completed, I hop off the examination table, pull my green shirt over my blue hospital gown, and hoof it out to the waiting room where my friend Ginny is waiting with my fifteen-year-old son. They are eating hot dogs from a street-side vendor and drinking sodas.

"There's somebody back there who *ate a rotten fig,*" I say, and we all start laughing. *"Four days ago!"*

My son leans forward. "I don't think you should laugh so much."

"He's right," Ginny whispers. "If you keep acting so happy, they'll keep us here forever."

"Why don't you two go sightseeing or something? This is wasting your whole day!"

But they will not leave me.

* * *

Last night, before the streaking pain shot through my left arm, causing me to sit down on a curb in my good skirt next to a hobo in a dirty Blue Jays hat, my son and I were on our way to *look at* a restaurant. This seems strange. Not to eat there, just to *look at it*. Bar Mercurio. A friend had told me it is a great place, tiny and atmospheric. But—what a dumb thing to do! We went out walking late at night just to *look* at something? Bar Mercurio was right where it was supposed to be, wrapped in a dim aura of elegance. We gazed a few seconds at cozy couples eating pizzas, then whipped around to walk back to campus. It sounds ridiculous, in retrospect. Take note: we *whipped around*.

When I said I thought I was having a heart attack, my son dodged across the street into a small grocery to purchase aspirins and bottled water for me. Then he stepped off the curb and motioned for a taxi. What a sensible guy. I would remember this moment later as "maturity occurring." Tears rose in my eyes on top of the pain.

As the taxi was pulling up, my son said, "Mom, should we get an ambulance instead?"

"No, I'll be fine."

The taxi driver was the one unfriendly Canadian we have ever met. When my son said, "Victoria University dormitories," the driver barked, "But which ones? Which street? They have a lot of residence halls!" *Grrr Grrr Grrr.*

We could not remember.

The pain recurred all night. I could not sleep for wondering if I should have gone to the hospital. At one A.M. I called the Tele-Health Live Nurse Hotline. She was very kind and wanted to make sure I'd been enjoying Canada. "Absolutely," I said. "Except for that swarm of aphids on Thursday."

"Very rare," she said. "I'm up here in Ottawa, but we heard about it."

I didn't mention the extremely high temperatures, humidity level, and smog because really,

Toronto is about the most wonderful city any of us will ever see. Any place that calls Joni Mitchell a "World Leader" on posters all over town is first class by me.

If my symptoms recurred, the Live Nurse thought I should go to the emergency room. Especially since I would be flying soon. We all know about blood clots and flying. We know so much we wish we didn't know. This is another reason why I love children's books. They restore us to the world before *excess knowing,* that keener, crisper world of filtered light and high hopes, that wide and beckoning field.

In the morning, when my left arm continued to hurt, my son was adamant about the emergency room. Our dorm neighbor Ginny agreed with him.

I thought, if I don't do it, and die, he will not only be sad, he will be *mad at me.*

I couldn't stand it.

* * *

Racing back to the bowels of emergency, I consider the resilience of the human frame. Already I *feel at home here*. This is truly weird.

The journalist calls over the striped curtain, "I heard you guys talking about William Steig. But E. B. White was *my man*!"

Jennifer and I agree that we can read the books or essays of E. B. White at any time and feel our minds have been *distilled*. Maybe White's books should be kept in every emergency room. "I am going to go see his boathouse up in Maine," I declare, having never thought of it till this moment. "I am going to stare out his little old window and see what he saw. Water, and rocks. I am going to make a pilgrimage. Anybody wanna go?"

The journalist is dismissed. The beautiful girl is dismissed. What was her problem? Jennifer won't tell. The Portuguese man is placed on an IV. When Jennifer leaves, he calls out to me mournfully, "My blood test is on that computer! I feel horrible!

They're waiting for my X-rays to come through on that computer. Do you ever feel like your whole life is on somebody's computer?"

I take the Dave Eggers issue to the X-ray room with me and, when the tall Scandinavian technician isn't looking, rip his Cuba story out of the magazine, fold it discreetly, and tuck it into my copy of *Bridge to Terabithia* by Katherine Paterson. I did not used to steal articles from other people's magazines, but somehow feel no guilt about doing it now. Perhaps because I am the only person in here without an official Canadian medical card and know that I am going to be paying out the bazooka for this experience—the magazine has become *mine*.

Jennifer says her favorite thing to do on a free day in Toronto is ride the ferry to Ward's Island, eat at a restaurant called The Rectory Café, and watch for the Queen Mums, a group of roller-skating octogenarians wearing vintage ball gowns, hats, and gloves, to skate by in a fragrant flurry.

"Are you serious? I'm coming back here. I mean, not *here,* but here."

The furious guy is sitting across the room from his mother's bed. He is reading a book called *Full Catastrophe Living*. Might we recommend *Stuart Little*?

Every time his mom calls out softly to him, he shouts, "I'm not talking to you, Mother! I've had it with you! I refuse to discuss *anything* until we get home!"

My son is so much nicer to me.

When I go out to see him again I will tell him I have had a revelation. I am going to become *a taxi driver in Cuba*.

After a vial of my own blood passes through secret channels onto the computer screen, and my other tests are analyzed, Dr. Ovens is able to tell me I have not had a heart attack at all. I probably have *a pinched nerve. Or acid reflux.*

In order to enter Emergency, I had to sign a mean

money page ("I will be responsible for all charges and deal with my insurance company *myself*") and hand over my credit card. I believe our insurance policy has a one thousand dollar deductible for escapades like this in foreign countries, though no Live Insurance Adjuster is available to confirm this when I telephone. Spending this much money would seem like a bad deal even if the King of Siam were paying.

Where is the King of Siam? Is he alive or dead?

The elegant pots of British face cream at Holt Renfrew department store don't even cost this much.

Dr. Ovens gives me his fax and telephone numbers when I leave. He stares kindly at me and urges me to "feel free to call." Oh sure. I can't imagine that. How does he keep his calm amidst the ringing beepers and pages and phones? I feel a pang as I exit, leaving all my new friends, wanting one man to get to his cabin, wanting the fussy son to love his mother before it's too late.

Ginny and my son are in a celebratory mood. "But aren't you *glad* nothing was really wrong? This is Good News!"

"Yeah, sure," I say. "This is super expensive."

My son has phoned home to Texas and left a message: "Dad, please call us as soon as you can. I *think* Mom is going to be okay."

Someday we will return to blow kisses to the Queen Mums. We will not waste our time. We will hail taxis for nice places only. We will eat at Bar Mercurio, not just look at it. If I have finished paying for the emergency room by then, I will buy a pizza for everyone in the place. They will have no idea why.

Criminal Handbags

"I AM NOT REALLY A TAXI DRIVER," SAYS THE
beautiful brown man with a perfect jawline and
perfect nose, screeching away from La Guardia's
taxi line. Of course not. He doesn't really work for
this company, doesn't have a driver's license, has
never, in fact, driven a car before in his life.

He has perfect dark curly hair, though.

"Hmmmm. So what are you really?"

"According to the New York police"—he turns
his head to glance at me—"a criminal. I deal in . . .
counterfeit handbags."

"You what?"

"Copies. You know, copies?"

Familiar gray skyscrapers beckon on the New York City horizon, but I have plummeted into an unexpected galaxy. "Hmmmmm. I don't know! You mean you imitate fancy handbags and use false tags?"

"Right." He pauses.

"Why?"

"It's a very good business. But I got busted, so now I'm a taxi driver, for a very brief time, I hope."

"But why would you do such a thing?"

"Get busted? I didn't want to."

"No! Why would you deal in counterfeit goods? Why would anyone?"

"Money, obviously. We can make seven hundred dollars in a day—that's a lot!"

I say nothing, so he continues.

"But it's also a service, what we do. People want cheap handbags that look like expensive handbags. We provide the service for them. "

He turns to look at me when I am silent. He also glances at my green purse. Hey! This is a real purse from Paris! My friend Katy gave it to me!

I say, "Ha. Service, right. You sell them on street corners next to the pretzel and falafel dudes?"

"I never worked the corners. My brother worked the corners. He didn't get caught. I worked the warehouse."

"Did you make the handbags yourselves?"

"Of course not. They're made in China. Fake handbags are a huge business in China. Fake boots, shoes, dresses—don't you know about this?"

"No. I really don't. It's not my area. I don't even shop. I mean, hardly."

The world of counterfeiting seems peculiar and abstract.

So many things we know not of.

I want to change the subject.

"Why not just invent your own cool handbags and sell them?"

He looks sad. "I am not a designer. I am a counterfeiter."

My driver who isn't really a driver and isn't really a purse maker, either, has a Middle Eastern accent, which also makes me sad. Does the Middle East need any more bad hype? I can't remember any of my Middle Eastern relatives even carrying purses. My Arab grandmother stuck Kleenexes and money into the open flap of pocket under the embroidery on her chest. My cousin carried money in her bra.

"How did you even get into purses?" Silence. Then, "Where are you from?" I add, "I'm half Arab," knowing some people don't admit to being Arabs anymore unless they feel comfortable with you.

He stays silent for a few seconds, then says, "Egypt. You been there?"

"Sure. Many times. Love it. Love the taxis. They drive like nuts."

He grins. "Why do you love it?"

"Well, I just love everything about it—the people, food, art, history, the Nile, Alexandria, the pyramids, the writers and music, the marketplaces, even the baskets sold on corners. I've had some great experiences in Egypt." We're passing old-fashioned diners and bridges and flower shops and wrought-iron railings, so I say, "It's as rich and mixed as New York City is, don't you think?" Again he doesn't answer, so I keep chattering. "Also I was there for a really bad dust storm once, working with a lot of kids in a library, and the trees started blowing over and hitting the building, and it was scary but exciting. The kids weren't scared at all. Red dust came into our hotel room where we were staying and coated all our clothes. We had to shake them outside from our balcony the next day. But it seemed so . . . elemental and . . . real, you know. Weather seems real." I don't tell him about sitting in the same booth in a café in Alexandria where the poet Cavafy used to sit, just by accident, and looking up to find a

Cavafy poem scrawled on a napkin and framed on the wall. He might not know who Cavafy is.

My driver has been silent for a long time. Maybe I made him homesick. And why did I bring up "real" when he was talking "counterfeit"? It must have been unconscious.

Finally he says, "Baskets sold on corners?"

"You know, those straw baskets people put bread and onions in. Some of them have lids? They smell really fresh, like wheat? " He is quiet. "You know those friendly men in long, woven, deserty robes who walk around with a hundred baskets tied to their bodies?"

I took two of their baskets home and put bananas and apples in them on the table.

"I remember them," he says quietly. Then he says, "Those baskets cost about ten cents."

"Yeah, they're very cheap." Another long silence, so I say, "Do you think you'll move back to Egypt someday?"

He says, "Maybe. I'm going to have to make a lot of money first. This is the land of money. When I was in jail, it cost a lot of money to bail me out. My fine was seven thousand dollars. I have to pay the bail money back to our partners now. Our handbag partners."

"They're not in jail?"

"No. They hid. One hid in a Dumpster. I don't think I could do that. Only I went to jail. But as soon as a few more months pass, I'm going back into handbags."

"Please don't."

"Why?"

"You'll get caught again. Maybe you'll go to jail for a long time. It's not worth it!"

"It is a great business. You just don't understand."

"No! It is a terrible business! There are plenty of legal ways to make money."

"Not fast like handbags."

"Do the people who buy the handbags know they are fake?"

"Sometimes yes, sometimes no. Some don't care. They just want the designer look."

"That is so sad."

"Sad?"

"To want something fake for a look."

He says loudly, "This is the land of the fake!"

"I thought it was the land of the money?"

"Land of the fake and land of the money both."

"And also the land of laws and it's not worth breaking them if it messes up your life, man! Also, it is not all fake. No, it is not." The next thing I see out the window is a tree. "Trees are not fake."

Silence.

What do I care about this handsome Egyptian and his bank account? I wonder if his mother is wrapping flat loaves of bread in a scarf at that moment and walking home through a crowded street. Does she have any idea what her sons are up to? Oh, the pain of mothers in this world!

I take a plunge and say something I know he'll

find strange. "You could be a model, you know. You could model for the real designers. Have you ever thought about that?"

He snorts like a horse.

"No way. Stupid job!"

"Yes, there's a way. Did you ever try it?"

"No chance. I'd be ashamed. "

I change the subject myself.

"Uh, do the Chinese go to jail, too? Is the production of the handbags in their own country illegal?"

"I think so. I mean, obviously the designers don't want us stealing their looks. I think there's a big investigation of it right now, and it's going to be on TV."

"Thank goodness you're driving a taxi at the moment. Please reconsider your destiny."

He pulls up in front of a pinkish hotel with a curlicue name similar to the name of the hotel I requested, but it's not the one I want.

"Hey," I say. "This is not it! This has *Plaza* in the name of it, but it is not the *Plaza* I want."

"Are you sure?"

"Very sure! Mine is by Central Park! The big old fancy one. I'm not paying for it, by the way. Someone else is paying. It's legal, though. "

"You say *Plaza*, I think *Plaza* this one." He pulls back into the traffic reluctantly. He really wanted me to get out of his vehicle.

I'm thinking, he took me to the wrong hotel with a spin-off name, but we wouldn't call it counterfeit.

All evening I'm staring at everything a little differently, thinking fake hair, real hair, fake fur, real golden and yellow flowers gleaming from a giant silver urn in the lobby. Is it real silver? Does the hotel worry about someone stealing it? Meeting one person can really change us. I can't stop staring at the rich businessman in a real suit that probably cost a thousand dollars snapping his fingers for a taxi, looking so irritated when it picks up a glamorous young woman clutching a lizardy-looking handbag, wearing a tight black sweater dress, instead of him.

Too Many Cars

My father has never liked the street where he and my mother live in Dallas. He says it is too wide, too crowded, too fast. My mother, on the other hand, very much likes their personal boulevard, with swift access to grocery stores, cafés, and banks. "Listen to the cars," my father says sadly when they sit together in the living room to watch TV in the evenings. "Listen to how many cars there are."

"I like them," my mother says. "They're going places. What's wrong with that? Action is interesting!"

On the night the first car crashed into their home,

they were both sleeping. My father leaped up, thinking the house had been struck by a tornado. "Or possibly an earthquake," he said later. "But I didn't really know what an earthquake would sound like." He stumbled groggily into the living room, flicking the light switches in the hallway and the dining room, but no lights came on.

He grabbed a flashlight and beamed it into the living room, moving it around like a searchlight. He could see into his office, with its nice paneled wooden walls, baskets of family photographs, bookshelves, and Oriental rug. He could see the front end of a vehicle in there, too. It had crashed right through the brick wall of his office and come to a stop in front of the Middle Eastern brass tray table.

"Call Emergency!" he yelled to my mother. "Get out of bed and call them right away!"

My mother said, "Why?"

Emergency said, "What should we send?"

My mother spoke groggily into the phone. "I don't know. Send everything!"

By this time my father was in his office with the flashlight, beaming it all over the crushed front end of a gray sedan.

My mother stepped into the living room in her raggedy flannel nightgown, but no farther, afraid she might trip over something. She kept calling out to my father in the dark, "What happened?" and he could only say, "There's a car in our house!"

She asked him, "Why won't the lights go on?"

The front door of the wrecked car opened and a middle-aged man got out. He was wearing a rumpled white shirt and black dress pants. He shook himself and stretched, looked curiously around the toppled room and said, "'Allo" with a European accent.

My father stared at him. "Are you hurt?"

The man said, "I'm okay. You sound nice." My father has a sweet little accent, too, from his early days of learning English by working for BBC radio in Jerusalem. He especially has an accent when excited or upset. "Where are *you* from?" my father asked.

The man said, "Croatia."

My father could smell liquor. The man stumbled toward him. My mother said, "I hear sirens. They're coming." She opened the front door. A police car, a fire truck, and an ambulance pulled up in front of their house. She said, "They're here!"

My father said to the man, "Hey friend, you're not a very good driver. Do you even know where you are?"

The man fell to his knees and wrapped his arms around my father's legs. He looked up at him and said hopefully, "Home?"

The emergency attendants entered the living room with their kits and hatchets, and my mother pointed at the man.

"No, buddy," said my father. "No sirree. You are

not at home. I think you are in the twilight zone."

After the man was examined and discovered to be completely intact in a physical sense (his drunkenness had made him supple and pliant), after a tow truck joined the party and dragged the vehicle out of my father's office, after the reports had been scrawled in the sharp circle of the policemen's high-beam flashlight, after my mother had announced, "I was having such a good dream when this happened!" and after it was learned that before driving into the house, the man had driven through the giant voltage pole that transmitted electricity in all directions, which was the reason none of the lights would go on, the man, who was being hauled down to the police station for driving while intoxicated, invited my parents out to dinner. Yes, he did. In his cozy European accent, he said it would be his greatest pleasure if they would, in the future, at some later, calmer date, be his guests at the restaurant of their choice.

My parents, being who they are, considered accepting his invitation, but after discussion, did not.

My dad had wanted a new office window for a long time anyway.

The second person who crashed into my parents' property drove through the chain-link fence into their backyard and flipped upside down, right beyond my mother's clotheslines. His black SUV overturned, spilling a vast CD collection of Mexican *cumbia* music into the grass.

My parents didn't wake up for this one. A policeman pounded on their back door, which seemed very creepy to my father when he finally woke up. He shouted, "Hey! Whoever you are, go away! I'm calling the police!"

"I *am* the police!"

The policeman had been chasing the guy for miles for running a stoplight.

My parents went outside in their pajamas. "This is getting old," said my dad to my mom. "I told you we should move."

The driver, also intoxicated, spoke no English. He offered no homecoming claims or dinner invitations. Much younger than the wayward Croatian, he kept his eyes turned down to the ground. My mom said he seemed embarrassed, as if he was expecting my parents to yell at him. But they didn't yell. They were too sleepy.

The policeman demanded the guy's car papers, which were hard to obtain from the glove box of an upside-down smashed vehicle. A tow truck came, flipped the car back over and dragged it away, leaving the music, receipts, cigarettes, and cigarette lighter in the dirt. The policemen hauled off the driver.

My parents were not happy about so many deep tire tracks in their yard. They were not happy about their crushed fence or being awakened so abruptly.

My father gave more speeches about moving to the country. But a man they knew in the country flipped over on his tractor, was pinned under it, and died. Vehicular disasters could happen anywhere.

Visiting my parents a month later, I saw the lonesome stack of Mexican CDs sitting on a side table. The driver's name, Antonio, was listed on one of his receipts. His place of employment seemed to be written on another piece of paper. It was a Mexican restaurant in a strip mall. I called to see if he still worked there. The manager seemed reluctant to give out the information. "But I have something that belongs to him," I said. "He lost it. I want to return it."

"What is it?"

"Music."

The manager put the guy on the phone and I stumbled along in my pedestrian Spanish. I found out how long he would be there that day and got my father to drive me over to the restaurant. "I can't see why you are doing this," my dad said at a stop-light. "Why do you have to get involved? You do the strangest things."

"I am a poet," I said. "It is my destiny to do strange things. But think about it! Your car is wrecked, you're living in a different country from where you grew up, and you need your music! Anyway, you're not listening to these CDs, and you never will. Why should they go to waste?"

My father gripped the wheel of his car. "I am the chauffeur for foolishness."

We said no more.

At the restaurant, I asked for Antonio casually, as if we were old friends. The manager looked me up and down and pointed to a guy dropping off a bus tub of dirty dishes in the hallway between the dining room and the kitchen. Antonio came out wiping his hands on his white apron and staring worriedly at me. He was thin and elegant looking, someone I would have had a crush on in college.

Maybe he thought I was going to punch him or lecture him about driving and civic responsibility, but all I did was smile, hand him the CDs, and say "Be careful, okay? Please don't drink and drive."

He looked at me without blinking. He looked at his music. He seemed a little stunned. Unexpectedly a small good thing had happened in his day. *"Adios,"* I said, and he said, *"Mil gracias"* in a soft voice.

My father and I drove home in complete silence, to his house on the bustling boulevard. A car had broken down at the corner and was blocking the turn lane. My father sighed, punched his blinker, and said, "God, I hate this traffic."

I said, "He seemed surprised when I didn't yell at him or anything," and my father said, "I don't want to talk about it."

After All That Walking

PEACE PILGRIM DIED IN A CAR ACCIDENT. Somewhere like Wisconsin. And for years she wouldn't even get into a car between towns. Very strange. A man was driving—I think he had offered her a ride—and he died, too. I don't think she knew him before their fateful journey. So, I guess it is not always true that we'll be fine when we entrust our lives to strangers. I guess nothing is always, perfectly true. But we're better off if we don't worry about it too much. If we do, we'll never be able to do much or go many places.

Our own small gray and nearly new car was totaled on a freeway in a bizarre pileup when our baby was three months old. Someone in front of us was fixing a flat tire and had stopped in the right-hand lane. Everyone behind him had to stop, too. A reckless driver behind us all didn't notice we were stopped and hit the whole lineup. What a mess. Luckily our baby was in his car seat in the backseat turned around facing the rear the way he was supposed to be. He ended up with glass in his diaper, but entirely unhurt. We ended up bruised and shaken and not afraid of flying, ever again. If this could happen on a highway only a mile from home . . .

Gifts

JUST PLAYING AROUND, I SING "LA LA LA"
from the stage of a nice medium-size theater in
mid-Manhattan. My voice blossoms widely in the
space as if it belongs to someone else.

A group of Arab Americans is rehearsing for an
evening event which will include drumming,
speaking, singing, poetry, awards and honors,
pretty clothes, jokes, and more music.

All I have to do is say a few poems and talk, but
how do I get into these things?

It is the question I ask every day of my life.

Stage managers are snacking on falafel sandwiches in corners.

September eleventh hasn't happened yet. The second war in Iraq hasn't happened yet. Many bad
things have happened, however—many bad things
in other countries which people consider the United
States at least partially responsible for. American
school rarely stresses these sorrows, though. We're
the good guys, and we like to be. Arabs still immi-
grate to the United States fairly easily, and
Americans visit the Middle East more comfortably
than they will in a few short years.

Mostly the Arab Americans are a pretty happy
group. We're drinking tea. We're wishing there
could be justice for everyone who needs justice. We
believe in culture and art and education more than
in politics. We believe in books and music. We pray
for no more violence against innocent citizens in
any country. Okay then.

Some of the presenters are going back to their

hotels to change clothes and take naps before the show starts, but I'm going to Greenwich Village to eat dinner with friends in a Lebanese café. I have a purple and black Palestinian hand-stitched jacket in my canvas bag—that's all I ever need to make me feel dressed up. A stage manager hands me two free tickets for the evening and says, "Give these to friends if you like."

It's exciting. Having free tickets to use or give away—that's the only kind of power I care about.

A yellow taxi rolls neatly over to the curb to let me in. The driver tips an ear to the small theater I've just exited. "I thought I heard music," he says. "Arabic music."

"You did," I say. "We're rehearsing for a show tonight."

"An Arabic show?" His head jerks around to stare at me. Yep, there they are. Those deep dark Arab eyes.

"Yes. Well, Arab Americans are in it, too. And

the star will be a brilliant elder poet from the old country who's going to be saying poems spontaneously as the music plays. That is the heart of the show. I heard he can go on for an *hour* without a script or anything, in the old Bedouin tradition. He makes it up." I say this famous elder's name, though I can't remember it now.

And the driver starts crying. First he tries to pretend he's coughing. But I can tell from the trembling of his shoulders. Then I see, in the car mirror, wet pools in his eyes. We're at a really long stoplight behind a bus. He wipes his eyes with the back of his hand.

"Do you know him?" I ask. "You must! Where are you from?"

"I am from southern Lebanon. I know the poems of this man you mention since I was a child. Yes. They are inside my body. I think my father heard him once and I also heard a tape of him. *Ya'Allah,* I cannot believe he is in the city of New York. I thought he was a hundred years old many years ago."

"Maybe he was. I haven't seen him yet, but they say he has some years on him. Say, do you want some free tickets to the show? Here you go!"

I throw the bright green tickets into the front seat.

We're in Greenwich Village already, and I'm hopping out at the café. The taxi door is open. I poke a ten over the seat, but he brushes it away. "*No!* You have given me tickets to hear the music of my soul! I will see the poet who lives inside my heart forever. I could never take money. Never, never!" He's yelling passionately and people on the sidewalk are glancing at us. Maybe they think we're arguing over the fare—which we are, but not in the way they might think.

"Friend, the tickets were free. Driving is your job! You *need* to take money!"

"Keep your money. I refuse it. Life is music, not money. Everything is music!"

* * *

My small jet had landed somewhat rockily, in a rainstorm in Santa Barbara.

I took a very deep breath. It is always so good to be on ground again.

Joe of Rose Cab was standing outside the airport next to his car wearing a damp wide straw hat and carrying an umbrella. He held it over my head so I wouldn't be drenched as I climbed into his taxi. He said, "Was your plane flight very rough?"

"It wasn't great," I said. "The pilot told us our flight would be 'deteriorating' for the last fifteen minutes. It gave me a headache. I like bigger planes."

The rain was coming down in strong sheets. Joe paused to go around large puddles in our lane. I could not place his accent. I noticed his meter was not running as we drove and asked him about it. "I am giving a gift," he said mysteriously.

Normally I ask people where they are from, but that day I was just wishing to be home in Texas asleep in my bed. Maybe he is Latino, I thought drowsily. That hat looks South American. Maybe he is from Paraguay or Bolivia.

At the hotel, which did not have a doorman, Joe got out of the car and carried my luggage all the way to the elevator inside the lobby. When I pulled out money, he put up his hand to push it away. "Later," he said. He touched the brim of his hat with an old-world courtesy. "Do you need to go anywhere else?"

I said, "Well, yes, actually. After I take a nap and recover." I told him my schedule for the next two days. "So, you'll come back and get me? Do you want me to pay you for all the trips together, or what?"

Joe just shrugged.

I watched him cross the lobby with a slight stoop, his neat cotton khaki-colored shirt tucked perfectly into his darker khaki pants. Honduras? Guatemala?

Hours later he was right on time, waiting outside

the hotel. He drove me across town to see Katherine, a second cousin of my mom's who had materialized in our lives only a few years earlier. A cheerful Christian Scientist in her eighties, she had told my mom and me that our long-dead German Lutheran ancestors were not nearly as goody-goody as my mom had believed them to be. They had all kinds of normal flaws. This was refreshing news. My mom had felt burdened by their piety all her life. Katherine told us we could give that up. She had baked an incredible moist lemon cake especially for us.

I was excited to see her again. When I stepped out of the cab at her place, Joe pushed my money away again. "No, no, you pay nothing. This is free. It's on me."

"But why? I don't know why you're being so nice to me!"

Joe smiled and shook his head. He promised to take me to work the next morning, too.

I felt mystified. I asked Katherine, "Do Santa Barbara taxi drivers ever refuse to take money from you?"

She said, "Never."

When she and I called a taxi to take us to a famous burrito restaurant, the driver took our money like any normal driver would.

The next morning Joe was sipping coffee in the hotel lobby as he waited for me. "Hello, Mr. Generous," I said. He looked away. Maybe I should have worried that he was going to do something bizarre, but he seemed so completely trustworthy. He wouldn't take money for that trip, either. "Joe," I said. "What's going on here? This is your job, right? So you *have* to take money when you drive people in your cab. Right?"

He shrugged. "I don't feel like it. Don't ask me."

So I said, "Tomorrow why don't you charge me double when you take me back to the airport, since I need to go there at five A.M.?"

He said, "Five A.M., four, it's all the same to me. I'll be here."

I tried to press a ten into his hand, saying, "This is just a tip," but he wouldn't take it. Very strange. So I made my plan. I'd slip a wad of bills into his hand at the airport and run away as fast as I could. Then he couldn't give it back.

At five A.M. the next day he was leaning against the taxi with his eyes wide open and his arms crossed on his chest, peacefully. When he saw me, he raced forward to grab my bags. In the car he said, "It's a beautiful morning, isn't it? Not like when you arrived. You'll have a smooth flight today."

We drove alongside the fabulous blue ocean. The highway was calm. Even the seagulls were asleep. I said, "It must feel great to live in such a beautiful place."

He didn't answer.

So I said, "How long have you lived here?"

An early surfer ran across the sand with an orange surfboard. I said, "Joe, where were you born? I've been trying to figure it out, but I can't."

He sighed.

Some days I forget where I'm from, too, and I realize it's not everyone's favorite question, but it's always a curiosity.

Then it struck me. The sadness in those eyes.

It was the same sigh I have been hearing all my life from my father, my uncles, my cousins, every one of them. How dumb could I be?

"I am from," he said softly, "Jer-u-sa-lem." He articulated the syllables very clearly, as if I might never have heard them before.

I slapped the back of his seat and he jumped.

"So is my father, Joe!"

He turned to look at me.

I said, "You are Palestinian?" and he nodded. I couldn't believe I hadn't recognized his accent. Maybe, after years of mingling with California immigrants, his accent had absorbed so many mixed-spice lilts into its nubby texture. Everyone was in there now. Every lonely driver and yard worker and dishwasher and maid.

He turned his head and said, "I thought you seemed familiar too. Hmmmm. I never tell anyone where I am from anymore unless they ask me. It is a sad place to be from these days. All days. Very sad."

I said, "Oh Joe, I know! Do you still have family over there?"

He nodded. "Everyone is there. Very bad days for them. My family is trapped. They can't move. They are too scared. It is like living in a prison. They can't come, they can't go. I wish they could move here, but it's so hard and they feel attached to home, even if the situation is terrible."

"No one knows the real stories," I said. "I mean, unless you are there or have been there. People read the newspapers and they have no idea of the things that go on." Then I said, "My grandmother lived to be a hundred and six in the village of Sinjil."

"I know that village well," he said, veering around the yellow cones that mean construction. "The village that used to be famous for grapes. They don't have them anymore, and no one knows why. Well, your grandmother had a long life. Hopefully she had a scrap of happiness in it. People aren't living that long now. People are dying in the streets. Too many young people ran away. No futures for them. Everything broke."

At that point his voice broke, too.

Joe, crying in the front seat. Me, crying in the back.

I repeated his words. "Everything broke," patting his shoulder over the seat, realizing he had been "giving me a gift" without any idea we shared the same ethnicity. Now it would be even harder to get him to take money.

But surely the whole point of him being in this

country was to make money to send home. Moments later I would press a fistful of twenties on him as he resisted, poking them straight into his pocket, then dashing away with my little suitcase on wheels, tears streaming down my cheeks.

But before that I said, "And here you are in California, all that trouble so far away."

"And here I am," he said soberly—Joe, who surely wasn't Joe to begin with, staring hard through the taxi window, careful to take the right lane to Departures.

Roses

A TAXI DRIVER AT WASHINGTON NATIONAL Airport points at my hat, then at his. We are wearing the exact same beige woolen cap with a rolled brim like Afghani freedom fighters wear on the evening news.

Of course, since we are in the heavily cosmopolitan metropolis of government and embassies and culture and art and history, we could be wearing all sorts of garb.

"I got mine in Peshawar, Pakistan, a long time ago," I say, grinning. "Where did you get yours?"

"Peshawar!" He waves his hand happily in the air. "I am from Peshawar! Why were you there? Why didn't you come to see me?"

We're pulling out onto the highway. I always love staring down into the Potomac as one lands here, catching glimpses of familiar monuments in the distance, imagining George Washington taking a little twilight stroll on his riverfront property with his hands folded behind his back and his white ponytail bouncing.

Cars, cars, cars. Virginia license plates mixed with D.C. license plates and their disgruntled TAXATION WITHOUT REPRESENTATION slogan. I don't blame them one bit. Anyway, it's better than New Hampshire's LIVE FREE OR DIE, which seems so melodramatic.

I say to my Hat Brother, "Well, I was visiting schools in your country! I was visiting marketplaces and poets. But you, tell me, do you like living here in this place of power?"

He says, "Yes, it's very nice, but it's getting too expensive."

I say, "I do not know what young people will do."

He says, "I do not know what anyone will do."

Then he asks, "How many rose bushes do you have?"

This is a surprise. *On me?*

"You mean at home?" I ask.

"Yes, yes!" He is whizzing around a bus.

Somehow I don't feel like the first person he's ever asked this question to.

I have to close my eyes and count them in my mind. There's the tall climbing white one and the raggedy-leafed yellow one and the sturdy red one and . . .

"Ummmm—seven, I think. Five big ones and two small. One of them is the child of the largest climbing rosebush in the United States, in Tombstone, Arizona. That one's as big as a small house. Mine is pretty big, too. The ancestor plant of the rosebush came from Scotland originally. The baby was brought to me in a coffee can. A couple of the rosebushes aren't doing very well; they might be dead. What about you?"

He turns his head proudly, "I have eighty!"

"*Eighty* rose bushes?"

"Yes, eighty here in America. My yard here is not very big, so they are close together. Perhaps they would be a little happier with more breathing space. And guess how many I have back home in Pakistan?"

"I have no idea. Tell me."

"Four hundred!"

"Goodness! So many! It sounds like a lot of work!" I say.

He stares at me in his rearview mirror disapprovingly.

"No, my friend, it is not work; it is beauty. Where there is beauty, work doesn't matter. You could work night and day, and the result would be more beauty. I have been in the United States only six years, or I would have more roses here. Of course there were the climate differences to learn about, and I don't have as many people to help me here. In fact, I have no one. Many times I find myself gardening by the light of the moon. Or the light from the post in the alleyway. I am thinking to buy some of those flaming torches I saw in a movie, to make light in the dark for gardening."

We're passing the old post office building with its ornate towers and cornices. The National Gallery with the World of Art tucked inside. "Who's taking care of all those rosebushes back home?"

"My friends and relatives." His voice sounds wistful now. "I send them money. Rosebushes are cheaper over there, of course. In the United States each one costs more. I buy them at the end of the season to enjoy the discount. Then I must tend them indoors till the perfect planting moment. Since my mission here was to make money to send home, I really can't be *splurging* as much as I would like to, so now I am working with small shoots, rooting them to have a new bush. I am trying to marry some of my bushes. It is a difficult procedure, but I have had a few successes lately."

I am always impressed by masses of flowers since I feel excited at home when even a single flower blooms. It takes a certain amount of bravado—and money, he's right—to plant masses.

In fact, we're passing giant beds of red and yellow tulips in the center of the median as we speak. Cities have plenty of money. I say, "Look, even in this wind, the tulips are keeping their heads on! That's amazing!"

He turns his head and smiles ruefully. "Of course, Madam, they are nature. Nature is very strong. They are doing what nature is supposed to do."

We reach the hotel, and I feel sorry. I would have liked to ask for gardening tips. Did he feed his roses coffee grounds as Mexican women do? Did he sprinkle ice around their roots to pep them up? Did the roses help him feel less lonely far from his country? Did he plan to go home someday? Could a few inhalations of rose scent help him feel the world was a friendlier place? Did he cut blooming roses for vases in his rooms? Or was he a non-cutter?

I pulled the rolled brim of my brown wool hat down dramatically around my face before I paid him. He lifted the brim of his hat as if he were tipping it gallantly. It was a very versatile hat. And the whole time I was in Washington, I kept wishing I were back home in Texas, puttering around my yard with the silver bucket and the trowel and the hose, taking care of my roses.

Backseat

IT WAS HARD FOR THE THREE-YEAR-OLD BOY to understand where his two great-great-aunties had gone.

They died, in their nineties, within three weeks of each other. He was used to them riding around in our backseat. We'd visited enchilada cafés, peach stands, flower stalls, yard sales. We'd go out in the mornings and stay gone much of the day, until it got too hot for them—stopping anywhere anyone wanted to stop. We'd look at the old tiled gate in Brackenridge Park. We'd feed the ducks. Once we drove around a little lake three times just so they could watch the sunset.

The aunts wore flowery dresses and gauzy blouses and stockings rolled below their knees. My son liked to feel the nylon. He tickled the aunties on their ankles and they tickled his belly. He would flop around on their beds and couches giggling, in between our jaunts into the world.

They all pointed out the window a lot. He rode in his car seat on the passenger side in front and kept his head turned around to look at them. They touched his long wavy hair, his soft skin. They were surprised by the cooing sweet burbles that popped out of their own mouths. Neither of them had ever had children of her own. Della said he was the first child she had ever loved and good thing he showed up, because she was almost ready to check out and how sad it would be to leave without loving a child. Leonora said, "That's my boy!" We were their personal taxi drivers.

To say "They died" didn't satisfy him.

"But where *are* they?" he kept demanding. "Why can't we go get them? Where are the sugar cookies?"

One day I actually took him to their graves, and he pounded on Leonora's tombstone as if it were a door. He said, "Come back here! Open up!"

I started crying. A pale feather flew in front of my face right then and I grabbed it and gave it to him. "Maybe this is a message," I said. He took it back to the car, but didn't hold on to it long. What kind of comfort is a feather?

We were out driving, just the two of us, a few weeks after the second startling departure. When people you love die, the world feels abandoned, even in traffic. We were looking for a place that sold tall expandable silver poles to hold up purple martin houses, and we had the name of the place scribbled on a small white scrap of paper. A hardware store man had written it down for us, as well as the pole's dimensions and the way to ask for it. Hardware lingo. And my son said it again, "Where are they? I want a taco!"

"Some people would say they're in heaven," I said. "Heaven is supposed to be a nice, peaceful, pretty place. I think they both believed they were going to heaven."

"Where is heaven?"

"I don't know. I don't know if I believe in it."

"Is it like the rose nursery?"

We were always driving the aunties to the south side of town to an old Dutch plant nursery, where they would exclaim ecstatically over plump roses, poke their noses into intoxicating petals, and try to find a cheap one. Della found a radiant red Don Juan rosebush once for ninety-five cents. I think the "9" in front of the dot on the tag ($9.95 regular price) had washed away in a rain. The manager, with a bemused expression, actually let her have it for ninety-five cents.

"Maybe. Maybe it's like the nursery."

"Why don't you believe in heaven?"

"I don't know. I never did. You can if you want to. I'll take you to Sunday school. They'll tell you about it. Some people might say the aunties are still right here, all around us, in the city they loved, right here in the air but invisible. That means we can't see them."

"I know that. Do you think so?"

"Maybe. That makes more sense to me. I still feel them in the air, don't you?"

He said, "I still feel them in the backseat."

We turned off onto Hildebrand Street and found the industrial warehouse called Electrotex and pulled into the parking lot. As I hopped out of the car, the little white scrap of paper blew up out of my hand in a sudden gusty wind. "Oh no!" I shouted. My son was unstrapping himself from his car seat and ran around to my side of the car to see what had happened. "Look!" I pointed at the small white paper blowing high into the air, whirling over the telephone wires, over the train track we had just crossed. Bells started clanging on the railroad poles and the train crossing bars fell down across the road.

"I can't believe it!" I said. "What timing! It's gone forever!" I wasn't sure I remembered the dimensions on it, either.

A blustery train with many freight cars rattled between us and the little piece of paper, now vanished into the parking lots of a popular Chinese restaurant and a rug warehouse. I threw up my hands. "Oh well! That's it! We'll see what we can do without it."

"Can we wait till the train passes and go and get it?"

"I think it's gone forever. Very bad!"

But we went into the warehouse and the smart man inside knew just what we were looking for when we said "purple martins." We didn't need any dimensions after all.

The man taped some brown paper around the sharp ends of the pole and asked if it would fit in our car. I said it could ride in the partially open trunk with a red bandanna attached. I would tie the trunk with a rope so it didn't bounce too much.

"Good idea," said the man. My son was fingering silver nuts and bolts in the big delicious tubs.

"Come on," I said to him. "We're outta here. Let's go make some birds happy."

Back at the car, while I was tying the trunk, my son saw the small folded white paper tucked beneath our windshield wiper.

"Mom! Mom! Look! They brought it back to us!" he called out, pointing.

It took me a moment to catch his meaning.

"They saw the paper blow away and since they are invisible, they could chase it. Look, it's their surprise!"

I was tongue-tied. Surely not.

I pulled the small paper from under the

windshield wiper, unfolded it, stared at it. Same paper. Same scrawl of dimensions.

How had this happened?

"Mom, it's our paper, right?"

Of course, we didn't need it now, but the paper glistened in my hand in the sunlight, a coded message saying something I couldn't quite read. How?

No one had been in the parking lot when it blew away. It was already high across the tracks and still blowing when we went into the store. The engineer could hardly have leaped off the train when he saw me pointing after it. . . .

"That's great," my son said confidently, climbing up and strapping himself back into his car seat. "Let's keep it."

I poked the key into the ignition with a trembling hand as he turned toward the backseat.

"Thank you," he said.

Acknowledgments

With appreciation to the Haystack Mountain School of Crafts, Deer Isle, Maine, and Stuart Kestenbaum, who steers so well.

Thanks ongoing to the Lannan Foundation.

Cheers to The Loft in Minnesota, especially Jerod Santek and Bart Schneider, and to the Poetry Trust in England and director Naomi Jaffa.

Thanks forever to my family and friends, especially Roberto Bonazzi. The paintings of Paula Owen and Roberto Munguia lift up my heart. The songs of Eliza Gilkyson help me feel brave and hopeful. Molly Ivins, oh favorite patriot, you kept us cheerful in the darkest days.

I'm grateful to Michael Nye, who never once said, "Can't you stay home more?" and to Madison Nye, who liked it when I left, and to Virginia Duncan, who does not have her own driver's license yet.

"Free Day in Toronto" appeared in a slightly different form in *Hunger Mountain*.

The "Joe of Rose Cab" section of "Gifts" appeared in a slightly different form in the *San Antonio Express-News*.